The Complete
Financial
Guide
for
Single
Parents

Larry Burkett

The Complete Financial Guide for Single Parents

VICTOR BOOKS

A DIVISION OF SCRIPTURE PRESS PUBLICATIONS INC.
USA CANADA ENGLAND

All Scripture quotations are from the *New American Standard Bible,* © the Lockman Foundation 1960, 1962, 1963, 1968, 1971, 1972, 1973, 1975, 1977.

Library of Congress Cataloging-in-Publication Data

Burkett, Larry.
    The complete financial guide for single parents / by Larry Burkett.
       p.   cm.
    ISBN 0-89693-094-7
    1. Single parents – United States – Finance, Personal.
    2. Women – United States – Finance, Personal.   I. Title.
HQ759.915.B85 1991
332.024 – dc20   90-20045
                                                        CIP

---

5 6 7 8 9 10 11 12 13   Printing/Year 97 96 95

CONTENTS

INTRODUCTION

In 1973 my family and I moved from Florida to Atlanta, Georgia. I had just left a business to join the staff of a national ministry as a financial counselor. It was during this time I began writing what later became a study on the biblical principles of handling finances.

A Christian orthodontist, Bob Lahr, invited me to share an office in his medical building. In exchange I agreed to counsel with some of his nonpaying clients. Our agreement was simple. He would accept whatever payment they were able to make, provided they would agree to meet with me monthly and stick to a budget.

I had done some financial counseling during my first three years as a Christian, although much of the time had been spent studying the Word, particularly the principles of handling money. By default I had become the resident counselor in our church on the subject of finances for two basic reasons. One, I had a business background in finances. Second, nobody else was willing to tackle the problems. I relied heavily upon the Book of Proverbs for much of the counsel I gave.

I learned the meaning behind an old cliché that says, "In the land of the blind, a one-eyed man is king." I didn't know a lot about what God's Word said about finances, but I knew a lot more than most of the other Christians around me.

After counseling with mostly middle-income families, I had concluded that the vast majority of financial problems were the result of mismanaging the funds that were available. In most instances, if I could just get them to handle their funds logically, they could easily get out of debt and even develop a surplus of money. As long as my counseling was limited to middle-income families or above, that premise held true.

In Atlanta I came face-to-face with a new set of conditions because many of the doctor's nonpaying patients were single parents, primarily divorcees who sought orthodontic treatment for their children. As I began to counsel with this group

I found some situations for which there seemed to be no solutions. In general they were living on incomes that were often less than half of the families I previously had been counseling. They had the same expenses for household items and additional expenses for child care that most don't have.

Small things, like minor car repairs, became major crises in their finances. Large items, such as orthodontic care, became insurmountable barriers that plunged them into debt and despair. The financial problems were compounded by feelings of hopelessness because of the situations they faced. Most had no choice but to place their children in day care in order to work. And most had to deal with the guilt of a failed marriage, on top of the other problems.

Over the next few years I learned a lot about the financial problems that single parents face and what others can do to help. There are specific responsibilities for the single parent prior to asking others for help, but without outside help, the long-term prospects can get pretty grim. The first part of this book is dedicated to discussing the plight of divorced, single parents and the solutions available to them. I address the majority of the references to single mothers for two reasons: *First,* there are many more divorced women who are parenting than there are men. *Second,* the financial needs of divorced women who are parenting are generally much greater than men. This is due to the fact that women earn approximately 60 percent of what men do in the work force. This difference is even more dramatic where the woman has reentered the work force after a prolonged absence.

I don't want to ignore the fact that many divorced men are also parenting, but if my counseling is any indication, their incomes are higher and their options are less limited.

On the other side of this issue are the divorced men who are supporting themselves *and* their separated families. Often their financial problems rival those of divorced women. All too frequently a man in this situation takes on a second family, resulting in financial disaster for both families.

The second section of this book is dedicated to the financial needs of widows. Again women constitute the bulk of this group. Prior to 1960 approximately 85 percent of all husbands predeceased their wives. The gap has begun to narrow a little during the past two decades as more women work outside the home and become exposed to the stresses that shorten a man's lifespan. But even so, nearly 80 percent of all surviving spouses are still women.

The average age at which women are widowed is 52, which means that their husbands were approximately 50 to 55 years of age when they died. The problems these widows face are enormous, both financially and emotionally. A common factor among most of the widows that I have counseled was the lack of knowledge about finances and the lack of good, unbiased counsel available to them. All too often a supposed counselor is actually a salesman in disguise. The last thing a recent widow needs is someone pressuring her to buy something or to invest.

I trust this book will become a resource tool to help widows understand how to manage their funds well and provide enough information to know how to evaluate the counsel they receive. I will try to cover all the topics I have found to be woefully lacking in the average widow's training, including how to develop a budget, how to probate a will, apply for veteran's and social security benefits, invest the available assets, and minimize estate taxes.

I don't profess to be an expert in single parents' finances. In fact, I delayed writing on this subject hoping that someone else more qualified would see the need and do it. However, after 17 years of teaching and counseling I believe the time has come to write down as much as I know. Singles need support and help, just as much as anyone else in our society, usually more. Perhaps this book will help to direct others into this vital ministry and help to mobilize the resources necessary to meet the needs that can only be met through the generosity of those with a surplus.

SECTION ONE

DIVORCEES

■ 1 THE PLIGHT OF DIVORCEES

Carol was married when she was just 19 years old. She and her husband, Bob, met in college and were married in June of Bob's junior year. In spite of the many objections by both parents, they were determined that the marriage was "God's will."

Five years later Carol found herself divorced and faced with trying to support her three-year-old son with little work experience. A bitter divorce left Carol and Bob at odds about everything from child support to who got the pickup truck. In reality Carol was emotionally better off than the majority of divorcees who feel like they have lost someone they really cared about. In Carol's case she had decided she would be better off without Bob. They had been fighting about almost everything, especially finances, for several years. We pick up Carol's story right after the divorce was finalized. . . .

With Timmy's child support and what I can earn we'll be able to rent our own place, Carol told herself. At least I won't have to listen to Bob complain about not finishing school because, "You went and got yourself pregnant," as he always says. I wonder if he remembers that it takes two to make a baby. "Besides," she said out loud, "Timmy's the only good thing to come out of this dumb marriage."

As Carol began her search for work she became acutely aware that the job market above $5 an hour was very limited and extremely competitive. After three weeks of searching she ended up taking a job as a waitress in a local restaurant. Her base salary was $2.50 an hour. Tips brought her income up to about double that amount. As would be expected, she had a difficult time making ends meet. The first month Bob's child support payment was late and she was unable to pay her rent on time. When the 15th came and the check still had not arrived, she called Bob's apartment. It was nearly 10 o'clock at night and she was surprised to hear a woman answer the phone.

"Is Bob in?" Carol asked timidly.

"Who wants to know?" the brassy female voice asked.

13

"This is Bob's wife . . . ex-wife," Carol replied. Inside she had a cold feeling, as if something had died. Without realizing it, she had somehow thought that Bob still would be faithful to her, as she was to him.

"He's here, but he's in the shower right now. You want me to ask him somethin' for ya?"

"Just tell him I called about the check for Timmy, please," Carol said, anxious to get off the line as quickly as possible.

"I'll tell him, but don't hold your breath, honey. He's still mad about havin' to pay for his truck. He said you'll get the money when he's good and ready."

Carol's hand was shaking as she put down the phone. She felt like she was going to throw up. She and Bob had argued bitterly, and she was even glad to be away from him, but she still felt the ties of marriage. She realized that somewhere inside she hoped they would get back together. Only first she wanted to make it on her own to prove to Bob that she wasn't the dummy he thought she was. Now she had the terrifying feeling that she was all alone — with her small son.

Things got more difficult for Carol over the next several months. She lived in constant fear of Timmy getting sick. With even the slightest temperature, the day school wouldn't let him stay and she would have to miss work. Twice in the last month she had to leave work early to get Timmy, and the manager had told her, "One more time, Carol, and you're fired. I need workers I can depend on."

"But I need this job, Mr. Hall," she had pleaded. "Timmy's not sick very often, and I know he's better now." Even as she said it, she knew that she had to keep Timmy on aspirin or his fever would return. She needed to take him to a good pediatrician, but there was never any money, or time.

Carol thought about taking Bob back to court to make him pay her more *and* pay on time. But the last time she threatened him he had countered, "Go ahead, Carol, and I'll take Timmy away from you. I know you're behind on your bills and you can't provide for him properly." This terrified Carol so greatly she was afraid to even call Bob again. She really was having financial problems and she knew she couldn't give

Timmy proper medical care.

One Sunday evening, Carol noticed that Timmy wasn't acting normal. Suddenly he passed out and began to convulse. She grabbed him up in her arms and raced out to her car. The nearest hospital was a private treatment center only a few blocks away. Carol dashed into the emergency room with Timmy still unconscious. The emergency room doctor took Timmy and began to work on him. Within a few minutes he was back to talk to Carol.

"Mrs. West?" he asked as he entered the waiting room.

"Yes, Doctor," Carol replied. "Is Timmy OK?" she cried out.

"Yes, he is. He just went into convulsions because of his fever," the doctor replied. "He has a very bad inner ear infection. How long has he been sick?"

"I don't really know, Doctor," she replied as she sat down in a waiting room chair. "It seems like a long time now, maybe four or five months."

"Well I'm concerned that he could lose the hearing in his left ear. I'd like to keep him in the hospital a couple of days and treat that ear with antibiotics. Do you have health insurance?"

Inside, Carol panicked. She assumed if she told them the truth, that she didn't have insurance, they wouldn't let Timmy stay, since it was a private hospital. So she lied. "Yes, I do," she said. "We're covered under my husband's plan at work."

"Good," the doctor replied. "Just give your account number to the receptionist and we'll check Timmy into the pediatric ward."

Carol took the old insurance card out of her purse and gave the account code to the receptionist.

"Mrs. West, we'll need to verify the insurance with your husband's company," the receptionist said as she took down the information.

Inside Carol felt like her heart skipped a beat.

Then the receptionist added, "Oh dear, since it's Sunday there won't be anyone at the claims office. I'll leave word for the day shift receptionist to check. But I'm sure it will be all right. Your husband is still employed at the same company, isn't he?"

"Yes, he is," Carol answered, without adding, "but he's not my husband anymore." Carol felt a flush of anger inside. Bob could have kept us on his policy, she thought, but he refused. The judge said he had to be responsible for Timmy's bills, but I know he'll try to make me out to be a bad mother, just for spite.

With Timmy safely checked into the pediatric ward, Carol went home in total mental exhaustion. The next morning she called the hospital to check on Timmy before she went to work. She was afraid to go by and see him for fear they would find out about the phony insurance and dismiss him. She asked for the pediatric nurse and asked how Timmy West was doing.

"He's doing fine, Mrs. West," the nurse replied. "He's asleep right now and should sleep for several more hours. Poor little guy, he was just worn out from fighting the infection."

"Thank you," Carol said with a rush of relief inside. "Please tell him I'll be by right after work. And tell him I love him very much."

"I'll do that, Mrs. West," the nurse replied. "And don't you worry about a thing, he'll be fine now."

Carol spent a fitful day at work. She was alternately caught between a feeling of relief knowing that Timmy was getting the treatment he needed, and the feeling of dread knowing that by now the hospital must have verified that she didn't have any insurance.

Time in the morning seemed to drag by as Carol worried about her son. But the afternoon seemed to fly by as she dreaded the confrontation she knew was coming when she went to visit Timmy that evening. Her mind conjured up images of the hospital having her arrested and the court taking Timmy away from her. By quitting time she was a nervous wreck. When she arrived at the hospital and asked where Timmy's room was, the lady in pink at the desk asked,

"What did you say his name was, dear?"

"It's Timmy West," Carol repeated.

The volunteer scrolled through the names on her computer screen until she came to Timmy West. Then she said, "Mrs. West, you'll have to see Mr. Harms, the administrator. Apparently there is some kind of error in your admission form."

Carol dreaded the meeting that she knew was coming. She walked slowly down the hall to the administrator's office. Knocking on the door she heard, "Come in please."

Carol introduced herself, "I'm Carol West, Timmy's mother."

"Ah yes, Mrs. West," he said, looking at the account notice on his desk. "It seems we have some kind of mix-up in your insurance. According to the insurance company, your son, Timmy, was dropped from the policy nearly nine months ago, when you and your husband were divorced."

"That's true," Carol admitted as the tears welled up in her eyes. "I lied because I was afraid they wouldn't admit Timmy for treatment last night."

"But Mrs. West, this is a private hospital and we're not equipped for welfare patients. The county hospital is funded for patients who are unable to afford medical care."

"We're not on welfare!" Carol snapped defensively. "I apologize for deceiving you, but I didn't know what else to do at the time."

"Well I'm afraid your son won't be able to stay unless someone guarantees payment on the bill," the administrator said with finality. "I'm sorry but that is the hospital's policy."

"Could I arrange credit with the hospital?" Carol asked pleadingly. "I don't want Timmy moved now."

"No, I'm sorry. Hospital policy requires that all credit must be approved in advance. However, we will accept all major credit cards for payment. Do you have one?"

Carol knew that she still had three credit cards from when she was married. But how will I ever pay them off? she thought as her mind raced through the options available. She then made a decision that was to drastically affect the rest of her finances. "Yes, I do. I have Visa and Master Card."

The total bill for Timmy's care came to just under $4,000, which took both of her credit cards to the maximum limit. The next month was filled with anxiety as Carol waited for the bills to arrive. In the meantime the brakes on her car began to make an awful noise. She continued to drive until finally the screech was continuous and the brakes smelled like burning rubber. She dropped the car off at the small garage near her work to have them checked.

When she returned to pick up her car that evening the mechanic said, "The bill on your car is $600, Mrs. West. You drove it too long on worn-out brakes and scored the rotors. We had to put on new ones."

"Six hundred dollars!" Carol shouted. "I don't have $600! How could it be that much?"

"That's what it took," the mechanic said rudely. "This ain't no charity work here, you know. We have a loan company that will lend the money for repairs if you own your car. You do own this car, don't you?"

"Yes," Carol said as she began to cry.

Inside she felt as if she had dropped into a pit of despair. Another loan, she thought. I can't pay the loans I already have. I can't even pay the rent this month. It doesn't seem to ever stop.

By the end of the next month Carol was shifting money from one creditor to another just to keep them off her back. Even without the credit card payments and the small loan company debt, she needed nearly $200 a month more than she made. One evening she returned from a long day on her feet to find a note from her landlord saying that if she didn't pay her rent she would be evicted immediately. Fearful of being put out on the street, she took the reserve she had been saving for Timmy's day school and gave it to the apartment complex manager. It didn't cover the entire amount due, but Carol promised to have the remainder by the next paycheck.

The next day as she dropped Timmy off at school she was met by the school administrator. "Carol, you're over a month behind on Timmy's bill now," she said. "If you don't get caught up by the end of this month, we won't be able to keep him any longer."

"I'll do my best, Mrs. Roberts," Carol said, fighting back the tears and despair. Oh God, she thought to herself, I wish I were dead. I never thought anything could be this bad.

That day at work one of Carol's regular customers came into the diner for his usual lunch. He was an older man who owned a successful package delivery business. He picked out his favorite booth. "What are you so down in the dumps about, Carol? You've been draggin' around for the last few days like you lost your only friend."

Carol was near tears anyway and she unloaded all that had happened to her over the last several months since her divorce. "I just don't know what I'll do," she said through the tears. "If they put Timmy out of the day school, I won't be able to work."

"Why don't you come and live with me?" he said. "I have a large home and nobody but me lives there. With what you'd save on rent and utilities you could make it."

"Why I couldn't do that!" Carol exclaimed indignantly. "I couldn't just live with someone I'm not married to."

"Well, I'm not looking to get married," Carl said bluntly. "I tried it once and I don't ever intend to make that mistake again. You think it over, Carol. If you change your mind, let me know. I think it would work out OK. Besides, what other choices do you have? You want to end up on welfare or have your ex- take your kid away from you?"

Inside Carol knew that the idea of living with someone just to pay her bills went against everything she had been taught growing up in her parents' home. They were Christians, although they usually didn't attend church except Easter and other special days. They had sent her off to Sunday School regularly until she was about 13. After that she had attended sporadically. Finally she stopped going altogether before heading off to college.

The more she thought about it that afternoon, the more she realized that she had very few other options. She might call her ex-husband, but it was unlikely he would help. She thought about calling her mom but that always ended with an argument. She had often said, "You married that bum, now you live with it." By that evening Carol had decided that she really didn't have a choice. After all, she told herself, it's not that uncommon today.

Unfortunately Carol's situation is being repeated with increasing regularity across the country. If the truth were known, many naive Christians would be shocked to find out that many divorcees, who are professing believers and even attend their church regularly, have established an immoral lifestyle based almost exclusively on economic necessity.

It is not my purpose to point an accusing finger at these women. Obviously it's wrong and most know it. What they need is a reasonable alternative. It's not enough to just say, "They shouldn't get themselves trapped in situations where they are willing to compromise." They need a workable plan and some financial help.

A PRINCIPLE TO REMEMBER:

God is your source, not people.

Do not be anxious then, saying, "What shall we eat?" or "What shall we drink?" or "With what shall we clothe ourselves?" For all these things the Gentiles eagerly seek; for your Heavenly Father knows that you need all these things. But seek first His kingdom and His righteousness; and all these things shall be added to you.
(Matthew 6:31-33)

Most adults today would agree that young couples want "too much, too soon." But few parents take the time and effort to discipline themselves so that their children will have a model to follow in their lives. Instead, once most couples can afford the "luxuries" of life they feel like they owe it to themselves to buy them.

I recall a story a friend told me about his wife during their first year of marriage. My friend, whom I'll call Gil, was a preacher's kid and had grown up in an era where the common viewpoint about pastor's salaries was, "Lord, You keep him humble, we'll keep him poor." This attitude was practiced with great diligence in most small churches.

Gil grew up resenting the stinginess of church boards and was determined to have the best in life once he was on his own. But without even realizing it, he adopted many of his parents' values, including a natural thriftiness.

His wife, whom I'll call Shirley, grew up in a very affluent family and never wanted for anything. Until she went off to college, she had never really dressed herself since her family employed several servants to assist in the menial things of life.

Anytime Shirley was feeling down or made a bad grade in school she would work out her frustrations by shopping at all the stores in her town. She merely had to sign her name for anything she desired and it was hers.

She and Gil met at a Christian college during the one semester Gil was there before getting expelled because of his flagrant disregard for rules. He commented that he only went there to meet a Christian girl. "Because I knew that Christian girls made better wives," he said in response to my unspoken question.

Three years later Gil and Shirley were married. Shirley's father, a strict fundamentalist, told her that once she was married she was her husband's responsibility and he stopped all funds.

Needless to say, Shirley was depressed over the sudden change from debutante to distressed housewife. As an ensign in the Navy, Gil had an adequate, but very limited income. One day, about four months into their marriage, Gil came roaring out of their bedroom to confront Shirley. "Shirley," he shouted, "what are all these bills for clothes and hairdressers?"

"Oh," she replied calmly, "I was feeling bad so I bought some things."

"You bought enough to equip an entire regiment," Gil yelled, looking at the stack of bills. "How in the world do you expect me to pay for these? You charged more than I make in six months!"

"Oh Gil, you don't understand anything," she said in her beautiful southern accent. "You don't have to pay for those things."

"Just how do you figure that?" he asked in obvious puzzlement.

"You just sign your name and they give you anything you want," Shirley said as Gil's mouth dropped open. "That's what I always did back home. It's like a courtesy the stores offer."

Needless to say it took Gil several long and often loud lectures to convince Shirley that such was not the case. He said that the biggest asset their marriage had back then was that Shirley's parents refused to supply her money and refused to take her back. She was forced to live on what Gil made and all credit was cut off. Gil knew how to budget because of his family background and Shirley quickly learned the value of hard-earned money.

One additional anecdote Gil shared was that after a few months the apartment began to look a bit seedy so he asked Shirley to clean it.

"How do you do that?" she asked. "We always had maids to do that."

"Well, we don't have any servants," Gil replied with that distant look that said, who trained this woman anyway? *You* have to clean the apartment."

A few minutes later Shirley appeared with a large bucket of boiling water and dumped it out on the floor. She then proceeded to mop it up with one of their bath towels. She spent the next hour alternately sloshing hot water on the floors, and then mopping it up.

Gil didn't have the heart to tell her that you don't put boiling water on wood floors to clean them. By the time they left the apartment he owed for the cost of having the floors refinished. "But," he said proudly, "Shirley kept the cleanest floors in the Navy housing complex."

Many young people, under the pressures of a less than ideal marriage, decide that it is easier to get out of a bad deal than to work it out. In truth, there are very few young couples who don't have marriage problems. With credit available the way it is today, a young couple can accumulate massive amounts of debt. Then the real problems begin. Without hesitation I can assure you that it's a lot of fun to get into debt. It's also a lot of grief to get out.

Perhaps the greatest asset my wife, Judy, and I had in our early married life was that nobody was dumb enough to offer us credit. Had we gotten into financial trouble, along with the normal interpersonal problems, I don't know if we would have made it. We had all the odds stacked against us. I was 19 and Judy was just 16. The first year of our marriage I was in the Air Force making about $125 a month. After the service I was in college and working as I could. We survived mostly on peanut butter sandwiches and Sunday dinner at her grandmother's house.

Several times in those early years either of us might have left, except that we realized that neither of us could afford to live separately. Later, after we both came to know the Lord, we realized that all marital problems can be resolved if both parties are willing to work at it.

In the case of Carol, the woman whose story I told at the beginning of this chapter, she thought life would be easier without Bob. Bob sensed Carol's attitude and built a shell around him to keep her out. Once that cycle started, it continued to escalate, with Carol more determined to leave and Bob withdrawing more. Ultimately Timmy became the total focus of Carol's attention and Bob was treated like an outsider, which he had become.

The unfortunate thing is that Bob and Carol's situation is being repeated throughout our society. As most divorced people discover, they don't escape their problems; they take them into the next marriage.

A PRINCIPLE TO REMEMBER:

Raise your children the way you should have been raised.

Correct your son, and he will give you comfort; he will also delight your soul.
(Proverbs 29:17)

■ 2 THE UNEXPECTED DIVORCE

It has often been said that it takes two to get a divorce. As many divorced people will attest, that is not the case in America today. While it may be true that both spouses had a part in the events leading up to a divorce, quite often the actual divorce is the sole action of one party and comes as a shock to the other spouse.

Looking back over the events leading to a divorce, a trained observer might note many signs that indicated one or the other of the spouses was getting ready to split. But unfortunately the unsuspecting party usually ignores the signs, or refuses to admit that it might happen, especially when both of them are Christians. After all, haven't we been taught that marriage for Christians is for a lifetime?

The Case of Ann and Harry

Ann had been married for nearly half of her 46 years to a man who seemed the epitome of stability. Harry owned a computer software company that he and Ann had started 20 years earlier. Ann stopped working in the business when their first child was born 18 years earlier. She continued to do the financial records out of their home until their second daughter was born four years later. Then she gradually lost contact with the business.

Harry and Ann were members of a large evangelical church in their community where Harry had served as a deacon several times. It seemed that their entire lives were built around their church and friends from church. Over the years several of their friends had marital problems and usually it was Harry and Ann they turned to for help. Several couples in the church publicly stated that they owed their continued marriage to Harry and Ann's counsel and concern.

Harry's business prospered, but it was clear that it would never be a major corporation and Harry would never be an international tycoon. They had often talked about the plans he had when they began the business. He wanted to have a platform to influence people for the Lord and, in fact, had often shared his testimony before business and civic groups in their community.

When Harry turned 45 Ann noticed a change. He often was moody and depressed. Sometimes he refused to get out of bed and seemed indifferent to the children. On occasion they would joke about Harry being in a mid-life crisis. Ann assumed it was a phase he was going through and it would pass.

Then one evening something happened to shake Ann's world. The phone rang. "Is Harry there?" the young female voice on the other end of the line asked.

"Yes, he is," Ann answered. "But he's in the shower right now. Could I help you?"

"No, just tell him Miriam called," the young woman said.

Later, as Harry came into the bedroom Ann said, "A young woman by the name of Miriam called for you a little earlier. Who is she?"

"Oh, just a girl we're interviewing for a job as a programmer," Harry said in a slightly irritated voice.

Ann let it drop but inside she thought, that's strange that an interviewee would call here about a job.

About a week later the phone rang again and Ann answered it, "Yes, this is Mrs. Stromm. May I help you?"

"No! Just ask Harry to call me when he comes in, please."

"Who is this?" Ann demanded.

"Harry will know who it is!" she snapped back. "Just tell him to call!" With that the phone went dead.

Inside Ann had a sick feeling that something was definitely wrong. When Harry came home, about an hour later, Ann met him at the door. "Harry, I believe that same woman called here again demanding that you call her. Don't tell me she's a prospective employee. What is going on?"

Harry put down his briefcase and said, "I'm leaving, Ann. I just don't love you anymore, and there's somebody else."

"Is it that young woman who has been calling here?" Ann asked as she fought back the tears.

"Yes," Harry replied. "Please don't make a scene, Ann. You must have known our marriage has been over for some time now."

Ann was devastated by Harry's comment. "No, I haven't," she replied. "I knew you were going through some problems, but I didn't think they were about us."

"I just can't stand it here anymore, Ann. You're a good person, probably too good for me. I just need some space. I'll be moving some of my things out tonight. I'll send for the rest of them. You'll be well provided for, don't worry."

"Is that all I mean to you, Harry, someone you need to provide for? What about our commitment to each other? What about all those other couples you told to stick it out even when they didn't feel like they loved their mate?"

"It just doesn't work for me," Harry said as he headed up the stairs. "I feel more alive when I'm with Miriam than I ever did with you."

As Harry exited the room Ann sat down on the couch in shock. She felt like her legs wouldn't hold her up anymore. What have I done wrong, she thought, as her mind reeled in panic. What will I do?

She began to assume the role that would be hers throughout the separation and ultimate divorce. As she went into the bedroom where Harry was packing his suitcase she said, "Harry, please don't leave. Whatever I've done to make you feel this way I know I can change. Don't throw away 25 years of marriage. Please!"

"Ann, it just doesn't work anymore. I care about you as a person, but I just don't love you anymore. I need to start a new life; you do too. You'll meet someone who will love you for who you are."

"But tell me what I have done," Ann begged. "I know I can change."

"You just never allow me to be who I really am," Harry said as he jerked away from her hands. "You strangle me with all this home life stuff. I've still got a life to live and I just need someone who is willing to go with the flow—like Miriam."

For the next several weeks Ann continued to call Harry and apologize for every real and imagined offense she had ever committed. She made the typical mistake that many frightened spouses make of taking on the guilt for Harry's unfaithful actions. The more she pleaded, the more remote Harry became.

"Ann, just stop calling me, please," Harry said callously over the phone. "I just don't want to live with you anymore. And it won't do any good to send Pastor Reed over here again. He was here yesterday and I told him I am not subject to his authority. God wants me to be happy. He certainly doesn't want us to be miserable the rest of our lives."

"Are you living with that young woman?" Ann asked in tears.

"Stop torturing yourself, Ann. Yes we're living together, but we consider ourselves married already. After all, marriage isn't just what is written down on a piece of paper. We're going to be married just as soon as the divorce is final."

As the days went by, Ann found herself unable to get out of bed in the mornings. In spite of herself she found that she was calling Harry and promising him anything if he would just come back. She had stripped away all the veneer of self-esteem and was groveling. Even her closest friend, Mary, tried to bring her back into balance, but Ann was living in fear now and couldn't shake it.

"Ann, you have to snap out of this," Mary told her. "You're not responsible for what Harry's doing. Stop demeaning yourself."

"I can't, Mary. I don't know what I'm going to do. Now Harry is saying that he isn't going to be able to support us after the divorce because the business isn't doing well."

"Well, is it?" Mary asked irritably.

"It was as of when Harry left. I suspect the young woman doesn't want Harry to support us."

"Ann, you need to get a good lawyer and make Harry do what's right. His girlfriend knows that you're vulnerable and is taking advantage of you. What has happened to your trust in the Lord, Ann? God hasn't given up on you just because Harry has."

"Oh, Mary," Ann cried, "I don't know if I'm a Christian

anymore. I don't even know if I believe in God. If there is a God, why would He let this happen to me?"

"I don't know the answer, Ann. Except that apparently God doesn't force any of us to follow Him. Harry had a choice to make and he made it. I know God doesn't like it anymore than you do, but it *is* Harry's choice. Your choice is whether or not you're going to make him provide for his family."

"But doesn't God's Word say that I am to honor my husband?"

"Sure it does. Just like it tells Harry to love and cherish you. But Harry chose to divorce you. You at least have the right to defend yourself. You aren't the offending party, Ann. You're the victim."

The next several weeks dragged by as Ann conditioned herself to the fact that Harry wasn't coming back. She would see him around town driving in a new red sports car with that young woman draped all over him. It made her heart ache, but it also helped to strengthen her inside. Then one day she discovered that she didn't feel quite so depressed anymore. She actually felt like getting up and helping the girls clean the house. All this time, she thought to herself, I've been so wrapped up in my pity that I haven't thought about the girls' feelings. That morning she asked, "Carey, Kristy, what do you girls think about what's happening to Dad and me?"

"Mom," Kristy, the youngest, said, "If I were you, I'd go over to his condo and slash the tires on his little car. He never bought you a new sports car, and you stuck it out during the bad times."

Carey then said, "Mom, Dad told me he wasn't going to be able to help me with college. It's like he doesn't want us to be his family anymore. That girlfriend of his is barely older than I am."

"Girls, I don't want you to hate your father. I don't understand why he's doing this, but we just have to learn to live with it and get on with our lives."

"Mom, he's going to try to cut out on you and leave you with nothing. You can't let him do that. Mary's right. You have to fight him."

"I can't do that, girls. Just because he doesn't love us anymore doesn't mean we can't love him. If I fight, the court battle will be nasty and expensive. I believe we have to turn Dad over to the Lord and accept that God is still in control. If so, He won't let us down."

"Oh get real, Mom," Kristy said with a roll of her eyes. "Dad's having the time of his life and we're barely scraping by now. Do you think he's going to care one whit that you'll be broke? He'll just buy another sports car to celebrate."

* * *

"Mrs. Stromm, I have no alternative but to grant your husband's divorce decree, according to the laws of our state," the judge said in response to her plea against the divorce hearing. He cites irreconcilable differences and has waited the prescribed time."

Ann was crushed again. It seems like every time I begin to feel normal again something else happens, Ann thought as her attorney put his arm around her. She had hoped that Harry would snap out of whatever he was going through now that his girlfriend had left. Instead he seemed to withdraw even further. It was like he had lost all confidence in himself. She had even heard that the business was going downhill because of neglect. She walked out of the courtroom single again after all these years.

Inside she was feeling that old panic that had ruled her life in the early stages of their separation. What will I do? She asked herself silently. I haven't held a job outside my home for 20 years. She looked at herself in the car mirror. "Well Ann," she said out loud, "I guess it's time to get realistic. Harry doesn't want you anymore. All you have left is your girls." "And God," a little voice said somewhere inside her mind.

The next few weeks were spent searching the want ads for jobs for which she might be qualified. Once, she even went so far as to apply for a position as a night waitress at a new restaurant. But when the manager had said, "I'm sorry, lady, but we're really looking for someone with experience," she had retreated back to her home, defeated and depressed. "I can't even get a job as a waitress," Ann said to her friend Mary.

"Do you want a job as a waitress, Ann?" Mary asked very matter of factly.

"I don't know what I want to do. I've been a housewife and that's what I enjoy. I like being with my children and maintaining a home."

"But haven't you worked on some committees and helped to organize several political rallies? If I remember right, you were pretty good at organizing and getting other people involved."

"Oh sure," Ann said as she poured herself another cup of coffee, "and there's a lot of demand for a middle-aged housewife to organize parties and rallies I guess."

"Who knows, there might be. Have you ever thought about starting a small party catering service out of your home? I'll bet there are a lot of working mothers who would hire you to plan birthday parties and maybe even some businesses that would want to have meetings catered."

Ann stopped and considered what Mary said. "You know, you just might be right. But how would I go about finding them?"

"Why don't you talk with Pastor Reed and see if he would let you put a note on the church bulletin board. We have a pretty large church. I'll bet you would get some response."

That week Ann went to see the pastor about posting a notice on the bulletin board. "Ann, I think it's a good idea. You really do have a gift of organization. I think you would do well with a catering business. You need to check on the necessary permits and licenses first though."

"Permits and licenses?" Ann asked in puzzled tone. "I didn't even think about that. What would they cost?"

"I don't really know, Ann. But I would imagine they're not too expensive. I'll call Bill Moore, one of our members who is an attorney, and see if he can give you some help."

"That's kind of you, Pastor, but I don't want to be a burden to anyone."

"Ann, you need to realize that you're not a burden. We're your family and we want to help you if you'll let us. It seems like you have shut the church out since you and Harry started having problems."

"I guess I felt like I didn't deserve to be a part of the church, Pastor. I know divorce is a sin and I wasn't even sure that I believed in God anymore."

"What you are feeling isn't unusual, Ann. Most people feel that way about a divorce. In many ways a divorce is worse than a death because the hurt often runs deeper. More often than not, the injured party takes on all the guilt. With the death of a spouse the hurt lessens over time, but in a divorce the hurt remains because the ex-partner is still around."

"I can't seem to let go, Pastor Reed," Ann said as much to herself as to him. "I know Harry doesn't love me anymore, but I still love him."

"Ann, I doubt that Harry even knows what he wants or doesn't want right now. I tried to talk to him several times but he won't listen. He keeps saying that God wants him to be happy. Right now he thinks being happy means being totally free to do whatever he wants. Nobody is that free, and eventually Harry will realize that. Don't give up hope. God is still in charge and when Harry is willing to listen, God will speak the truth in his ear."

"I don't know, Pastor. He acts like he doesn't care about his family at all."

"Ann, Harry is going through what I've heard called the mid-life crisis. It's something that a lot of men experience in their 40s or 50s. They're trying to recapture their youth. One day he'll wake up and realize that he's being stupid. If you're open, he may even try to ask for your help. In the meantime you just need to get on with your life and let God do whatever has to be done in Harry's life."

"I'll certainly try, Pastor. But right now I feel like I need to get busy. Harry's business is doing poorly and he is not sending us enough to live on."

Ann posted her notice on the church's bulletin board after she applied for the proper licenses and permits. Her first client was the attorney who helped her. He asked her to cater an office party for a senior partner who was retiring. The party was a huge success and Ann's business was launched. Within six months she had three part-time people working for her and was booked up several weeks in advance.

She heard from several people at church that Harry's business continued to decline and that he had lost his biggest customer due to an equipment breakdown that had delayed a vital software package from being completed on time. Ann's business still wasn't generating enough income to support her and the girls, but the trend was improving monthly.

* * *

Ann became a success story. She was one of the fortunate few divorced women who was able to generate most of her income needs without struggling in the job market. However, most women in Ann's situation find themselves in desperate straits financially and in need of outside help just to make ends meet. The resources needed are readily available within most local churches. The unfortunate truth is that most Christians have been blinded to the needs of single parents. They somehow think that the "government" provides all their needs. Not so. Single parents don't need welfare; they need friends who care. The only long-term solution to the dilemma of single parents is a good job with adequate pay.

That means facing the job market.

A PRINCIPLE TO REMEMBER:
God provides for those who are faithful.

Offer to God a sacrifice of thanksgiving, and pay your vows to the Most High; and call upon Me in the day of trouble; I shall rescue you, and you will honor Me.
(Psalm 50:14-15)

■ 3 FACING THE JOB MARKET

The first time a divorcee with children came into our offices for financial help I saw the reality of "too much month and too little money." She came at the encouragement of her pastor, whom I had met while teaching a seminar at his church. Nearly 20 percent of his congregation was made up of single parents, primarily divorcees. They were attracted to his church because of a strong singles' support group that was started by a church member who had herself been divorced in her mid-30s. She understood the plight of single parents as only one who has experienced the trauma first-hand can. After her divorce she lost her home, car, and credit. She was faced with the prospect of raising three children on an inadequate salary and $300-a-month child support.

The liberal idealogies of the late '60s and '70s had "freed" women from the confines of being treated as the weaker sex. Along with the new freedom also came the trend in the courts to grant insufficient child support, no alimony, and little or no pressure on husbands to meet the material needs of their families.

Lest I be accused of misrepresenting the facts, let me hasten to say that many men, perhaps most, want to provide for their families. Some do so adequately, even after a divorce. But unfortunately, many do not. Statistics verify that nearly 90 percent of all divorced men remarry within five years. With a new family to support, the incentive to support the previous one wanes. Unless the first spouse is willing and able to seek court action, the monthly payments become sporadic and often less than the assignment.

Sally's Story

Sally, who began the singles' support group mentioned earlier, had been married 10 years before her divorce and had worked most of that time as a clerk with a national insurance company. Her salary was just about half of her husband's, which was OK while they were married because her income allowed them to buy the things that a single income would not have—a second car, two vacations a year, etc. This all changed abruptly when the divorce was finalized. Her husband was directed to pay the credit card debts (nearly $4,000) and to make the payments on her car for six months, in addition to $300 a month in child support.

Within six months he defaulted on the credit card bills and Sally received notification that she was being sued for the debts. She contacted an attorney who forwarded a copy of the divorce decree assigning the debts to her husband. That stopped the lawsuit threats but a few weeks later she received notice from the credit collection agency that her file had been turned over to a credit reporting agency. Her credit rating was lowered to the "bad debt risk" category and from that point on she had no access to further credit and her card was canceled.

Her husband began to get later and later on his payments for child support. Then one month the check didn't come at all. She called his apartment only to find that he had moved, lock, stock, and barrel. Being in construction, his work location often varied and Sally was unable to locate him.

Month by month she fell further behind on her normal bills. One month she was juggling the electric bill, the next it was the gas, and so on. She lived in dread of the day the car would break down, or one of the kids would get sick, because she knew she did not have the money to pay. She thought about taking on a second job at night but the cost of child care would have been nearly as much as she was making. Also she could already see the influence that the lack of supervision was having on her children. She feared that without some parental supervision they would begin to get into real trouble.

One month the inevitable happened: her car broke down. Fortunately it wasn't anything major, just a bad alternator. But the repair bill was nearly $100. The shop was adamant about being paid before she could have the car.

"Listen, lady, things are tough all over," the shop manager said caustically. "But my orders are absolute—nobody gets their car without paying—in full. If you want your car you'll have to pay."

"But I don't have that much," Sally pleaded. "Couldn't I just make payments for a couple of months? I'll pay them, I promise."

"If you want to take out a loan, go to a bank. This is a car repair shop, not the Salvation Army," the manager said as he stuck her keys in his drawer.

In desperation Sally went to her boss, who managed their local office. "Mr. Lyle, I need an advance on my salary again," Sally said as she slumped into a chair.

"What's the problem now, Sally?" he asked sympathetically. He had several women just like Sally working in the office. He knew finances were a constant struggle for them, and bent the rules whenever possible to help them out.

"My car wouldn't start this morning so I took it into the shop near where I live. It's going to cost nearly $100 to get it out, and I just don't have the money right now."

"Sally, you seem to always be running behind anymore. Isn't you husband paying you anything?"

"No, sir. The last check I received was over six months ago, and it bounced."

"Have you considered taking him back to court?"

"Yes, but no one even knows were he is. My attorney says it would be useless unless I want to swear out a warrant for his arrest. I don't even have the $50 it would take to do that."

"Sally, I really wish I could help, but the company has very strict policies against advancing money to employees. The branch manager sent me a memo just this week directing me to stop all salary advances—I'm sorry. But my church might be willing to help. We have a benevolence fund for needy people."

The words *needy people* struck Sally like a hammer. "But I'm not a beggar, or a street person. I don't need welfare," Sally said defensively. "I can take care of my own family."

"Sally, people helping people isn't welfare, and I don't mean to imply that you're a street person. But you need help and others with a surplus are willing to help honest people in need. Any one of us could be in a similar situation."

"But why would your church help me?" Sally asked as she

sat back down. "I'm not a churchgoer and I'm not especially interested in religion. I went to Sunday School a long time ago, but I didn't get much out of it."

"You don't have to attend church or be a Christian to qualify for help. Jesus said that we should care for the needy around us. I assure you, you won't have to join the church or even go to church unless you want to. But our rule is that we won't help anyone unless they talk to one of our volunteer counselors. All we want to know is that you're handling your finances as well as possible."

"Thanks, but I don't think so," Sally responded as she got up to leave. "We'll be OK. Something will work out."

"That's up to you, Sally. But if you feel like you do need help I'll be glad to call the church for you."

I sure don't need anyone telling me how I should spend my money, Sally thought as she went back to her desk. And we don't need welfare — from the church or otherwise.

Out of desperation Sally dipped into the utilities account she had set up to ensure that the lights and gas would always be paid. The company had sent her notice that the next time her account was overdue 10 days or more they would turn her utilities off. We have just enough to make it, she thought to herself . . . *if* we don't have any more problems. By the time I get paid again the utilities will be only nine days past due. I'll drop by the office and pay them in cash.

A few days later Sally arrived at home to find another crisis waiting for her. "Mom, the mailman brought you a registered letter," her daughter yelled from her bedroom. "It's on the table."

An involuntary shudder went through her as she opened the letter. What now? she thought. Doesn't it ever let up? "Oh no!" she let out as she read the letter.

"What's the matter, Mom?" her daughter asked, running out of her room at her mother's outcry.

"It's my car insurance. I completely forgot about it, now it's been canceled. The state patrol says I've got to bring in my car tags and park the car until I can get insurance."

"Mom, how are we going to get around without a car?"

Sandy asked in a typical teenager's manner. "Mom, we need a car!"

"I know we need the car, Sandy. I don't need you to tell me that we need the car!" Sally snapped back. "And why don't you help clean this place? You and your brother make a mess and expect me to clean up after you. I'm sick and tired of being treated like a maid."

"OK, Mom," she responded, obviously hurt. "You made your point, don't take your frustration out on me."

Sally went about the task of preparing dinner, but inside she was in turmoil. What am I going to do? she asked herself. I've got to have a car or I can't work. Even with the utility money I don't have enough to pay the insurance. And if I don't pay the utility bill they'll turn the lights and gas off, then what would we do?

The next day she went back to the manager's office. "Mr. Lyle, I need help," she said despondently. She went on to tell him about the insurance and the letter from the police. "What will I do?" she asked pleadingly. "It's like I'm in a pit with no way out. Last night I even snapped at my daughter. If the pressure gets any worse I'm afraid I might crack up."

"Are you willing to talk with a counselor from our church to see if we can help?" he asked politely.

"I guess so. I don't have anywhere else to turn. I feel like I'm trapped."

"I don't want you to feel like you're being forced to do something you disagree with, or that I'm trying to bribe you into seeing a counselor, Sally. I know from past experience that our counselors won't put any pressure on you as far as the church is concerned."

"OK, I guess I really don't have any alternatives. Would you call and make me an appointment as soon as possible?"

"I'll do it right now," he said as he picked up the phone. He rang the church office and talked with the pastor's secretary. "Elizabeth, this is Bob Lyle. Could you tell me who is handling the benevolence ministry this week? Ralph Miller? Good, I'll call him now."

He then called the volunteer who was in charge of the

benevolence program for the week. He explained a little of the situation and then put Sally on the line.

"Hi, Sally," Ralph Miller said cheerfully. "I understand you're having some temporary difficulties. We would like to help if you'll let us. Could you come by my office about noon? I'll have my wife meet us here and we'll take you out to lunch."

"Yes, of course," Sally replied before she had a chance to think of anything else.

"Good, I'll see you here about 12 or so. Bob can give you directions."

At noon a nervous Sally drove up to the real estate office of Ralph Miller. "Oh, it's *that* Ralph Miller," Sally said out loud to herself. "I wonder why he would take time out of his schedule to see me? He's one of the biggest developers in the city." Entering the large lobby Sally made her way to the receptionist's desk. "I'm here to see Mr. Miller, please," Sally said meekly.

"Yes, Mrs. Mulkey, he's expecting you. Have a seat and I'll tell him you're here."

A few minutes later Ralph Miller appeared. "Sally, welcome," he said. "Please come into my office. We decided to have some lunch brought in so it would give us a little more time to talk."

"Thank you, Mr. Miller. I know you're a very busy man and I apologize for bothering you."

"Nonsense, Sally, and it's Ralph. You're the most important agenda we have right now. This is my wife, Rachel. Tell us a little about your problem."

Sally began to pour out her story, beginning with the problems she and her husband, Paul, had that ultimately led to a divorce. She went on to explain that Paul had stopped supporting them altogether and she had no idea where he was presently.

"Would you ever consider getting back together with your ex-husband?" Rachel Miller asked.

"No," Sally said emphatically. "My financial situation may be worse but my life is a whole lot better since he's gone."

"I understand how you feel," Rachel replied. "I felt the same way about my first husband."

"You were divorced?" Sally said before she thought about it.

"Yes I was, Sally. But God in His mercy sent me a new husband. You see, my first husband was an alcoholic who would beat me up when he came in drunk. We had a beautiful home and lots of things, but our lives were a living hell."

"I know how you felt," Sally said honestly. "We didn't have a lot of things, except credit. But my husband drank too much and chased women. How did you meet Mr. Miller?"

"I met him after the Lord touched his life, Sally. You see, Ralph was my first husband too."

"You mean he's the same man who used to beat you up?" she asked in disbelief.

"Yes I was, Sally," Ralph Miller said. "I'm not proud of it, but I believe I'm a new man now. And for the last 10 years we've had a great marriage. Don't give up hope. God is still at work. I'm a walking testimony to that fact.

"Now, to deal with your problems. As I see it you have an immediate need to get your insurance paid and the utility bill caught up."

"Yes, sir. But I think I can take care of the utilities by the next paycheck," Sally said.

"Perhaps so, but that's going to put you constantly behind," Rachel added.

"It seems like I'm always behind," Sally replied. "I just can't make enough to get caught up before the next crisis hits."

"We see a lot of single parents who say the same thing, Sally. It's like an epidemic in our country today as the family continues to disintegrate through divorce and neglect. We would like to help you if you'll allow us to."

"I don't want any welfare," Sally said emphatically. "I just have a temporary problem and I'm willing to pay back any money that is loaned to me."

"Sally, I suspect you're not facing reality yet. Unless your husband is willing and able to help, you're probably facing a continuing problem—at least until your income improves. We're not in the lending business, and you don't need a loan. That would just cause you more grief when the notes came due. What I would like to do is take a look at your whole financial situation and go to the church with a proposal for how we can help."

"But I don't want my problems spread all over the church," Sally said defensively. "Maybe this just won't work out."

"Now Sally, you need to accept the fact that we're here to help," Rachel said. "The whole church won't know about your situation, only the benevolence committee, and I'll guarantee you that they won't mention this to anyone."

Sally, Ralph, and Rachel spent the better part of the next hour going over Sally's finances in detail. When they had finished, Ralph said, "I'm glad to see you have managed your funds well, Sally. Your problem is, you don't make enough income to meet all of your monthly expenses. I'm going to recommend to the committee that we pay your car insurance and supplement your income by $100 a month for at least the next year."

"You mean your church would do that for me? But I'm not even a member."

"You don't have to be a member of our church to need help, Sally. The Lord said that we are to help those in need. That was not limited to any particular group. By the way, we have an excellent single parents group at our church. If you ever feel like you just need someone to talk to who has been down the same road, I would encourage you to contact them."

"Oh, I'm not much for going to church," Sally said looking down.

"You don't have to go to church, unless you want to. The parents' support group meets on Tuesday evenings at one of their homes. They usually have several people from outside the church who attend."

"I'll think about it," Sally said as she tried to accept what she had been hearing. "Can I ask you something?"

"Sure, go ahead," Ralph replied.

"Why are you and Rachel doing this? I mean, what do you get out of it?"

"Just the satisfaction of helping a fellow human being who is in need," said Ralph as he settled back into his chair. "You see, someone took the time to help me when I was down and out and I just want to repay the debt by helping others. Maybe one day you'll have the chance to help someone else too."

Maybe I will, Sally thought to herself. I've been so wrapped up in my own problems that I forgot there are probably people out there with bigger problems than mine.

True to his word, Ralph approached the benevolence committee with Sally's situation. Unknown to her, Ralph and Rachel committed to covering Sally's needs themselves and took on the responsibility to meet with her monthly to see how she was doing.

Over the next month Sally's financial situation improved. The additional funds helped meet some of the nagging budget items that she could never meet out of her own income. In addition, Ralph made it a point to see if he could track down her husband. He did so by contacting several friends in the building business. It turned out that he was working as a carpenter on a commercial project being built by one of Ralph's friends. One day after work Ralph and a member of the church deacon board knocked on the door of Paul Mulkey's trailer.

"Yeah, what do you want?" Paul asked rudely as he opened the door just a crack.

"My name is Ralph Miller, Paul. We would like to talk to you about your wife, Sally."

"Did she send you here?" he asked abruptly as he started to close the door. "You tell her if she doesn't want to live with me, I'm not paying her anything."

"Wait, Paul. Sally doesn't know we're here and she doesn't know where you live. You must realize you're in defiance of a court order to support your family. You don't want the police to show up here and arrest you, do you?"

Paul opened the door just a crack more so he could see the two men better. "You mean you haven't told the police where I am?"

"No, Paul," Ralph replied. "And we don't want to do that if possible. Will you let us in so we can talk?"

Paul stepped back from the door and allowed the two men to come inside. The room was a total mess and furnished with only a threadbare sleeper sofa. "It's all I can afford," he said defensively. "I don't make much as a carpenter right now."

Ralph began the conversation by getting right to the heart of the matter. "Paul, I represent a local church that has been trying to help Sally meet her living expenses. We're not here to accuse you, but just to find out who you are and why you're trying to avoid your responsibility to your family."

"Listen!" Paul shouted, "She left me. It's been just as hard for me as it has for her. She could come back anytime. But no, she said she would never come back. So let her do without for awhile too. Maybe she'll see it wasn't so bad before."

"Why do you think Sally left you, Paul?"

"Because she always wanted more than I could give her. She was always bringing up other people who had a lot more than we did. I did OK by her. After all, I'm not a college grad. I'm a construction worker. Sometimes I make a lot and sometimes I don't."

"Paul, Sally said the primary reason she left was that you drank too much, especially when you were out of work."

"Well, maybe I did," he said, calming down a little. "But I felt like I was never good enough for her anyway. She may be smarter than me but I'm still the man of the house."

For nearly two hours Ralph discussed the situation with Paul. Ralph then asked if he would be willing to meet with Sally and a counselor to try to work out their differences.

"I don't think she'll meet with me," Paul growled. "She might even have me arrested."

"Paul, if Sally wanted you arrested she would have already done so," Ralph told him. "After all, if we could find you, the police could too. Besides, you don't want to spend the rest of your life hiding from the police, do you?"

"No, and I do have most of the money I owe her. I put it in a savings account each week. I'm not a deadbeat like she thinks. I care about my children. I guess I just let my anger at Sally make me do something dumb. You tell her I'll start sending as much as I can each week and I'll send what I owe now by the end of the month."

"Why don't you call her and tell her yourself?" Ralph suggested.

"I can't do that. Every time we talk she gets down on me about something. I can't argue with her; she's smarter than I am."

A few days later a check for $800 came in the mail to Sally. As she opened the letter she knew that Ralph must have had something to do with it and she called him. "Mr. Miller, this is Sally. I just got a check from Paul, and he says he'll begin supporting us regularly. Did you make him do this?"

"No, Sally, I really didn't. We did go to see him but he told me he had been saving the money for you. It isn't that he didn't want to support his family. He was hurt over the divorce and was trying to get back at you."

The bottom line of Sally's story is that she and Paul were remarried about a year later. They still had many difficulties to work out, but the one factor they shared together was the acceptance of Jesus Christ as their Savior. Both were led to the Lord after attending counseling provided by the church. Sally's other story begins there.

She felt a conviction about helping other women in her circumstances so she decided to begin a full-time support group for single parents. She accomplished two goals: (1) she made a commitment to be totally dependent on Paul's income, and (2) she was able to minister to others in need in her time of "plenty."

One of the immediate needs she recognized was the plight of new divorcees merging back into the work force. Many women who are divorced are either unemployed or underemployed. Many lack the basic job skills to provide for themselves and some are in situations that prohibit them from being reunited to their former spouses. Usually this is because of a remarriage, physical abuse, imprisonment, or the like. Obviously the goal of any Christ-oriented program should be to reunite families, but statistically the percentage of those who are reunited is less than 5 percent.

A PRINCIPLE TO REMEMBER:
God uses people to help people.

At this present time your abundance being a supply for their want, that their abundance also may become a supply for your want, that there may be equality.
(2 Corinthians 8:14)

What Happened to Kia
Kia came to my office as a result of being counseled by Sally. She was 21 years old, with a two-year-old son. She had gotten married in her junior year of college to a young man she had met only six months earlier. Their parents helped to set them up in a small apartment near the college. Her new husband, Matt, took a job delivering newspapers to pay their basic expenses. Although on birth control pills, Kia got pregnant within six months of their marriage, and subsequently had to drop out of college because of morning sickness. Matt struggled on for another semester, but the pressures of the coming birth and ever increasing struggles in their marriage forced him to drop out too.

Once they were out of school and had left the friends they knew, their relationship continually declined. Even before the baby was born Kia was spending as much time at her parents' house as she was with Matt. Unknown to Kia, Matt had developed a relationship with a young woman at the record store where he was working. Just before the baby was born he told her that he was in love with the other woman and he was leaving. He immediately moved out and told Kia to file for divorce, which she did.

For a short while she lived with her parents, but she and her mother argued about the care of her baby and she decided to move out. Her dad paid the first month's rent on an apartment and the utilities deposits. She then began her search for a job to supplement the $150-a-month child support from Matt.

With few job skills and the need for at least $1,000 a month in income she received a rude shock — no offers. Ultimately she took a job in a retail store in the mall making $1.50 an hour, plus commissions. The job required her to work from 9 A.M. to 6 P.M., Tuesday through Saturday. Kia was once again forced to ask her mother to keep her son.

Within two months it was obvious that she was not going to be able to make enough to hire a baby-sitter or put her child in a daycare center. Even worse, she and her mother were again at odds over how to raise her son. One evening as she went to pick him up she heard her parents arguing. Her father was shouting at her mother that he didn't intend to raise another child, and it was time for Kia to take her own kid home.

She stood outside the door for a long time just trying to shake the fear that rose up inside her. Inside she knew that what her father was saying was right. She had married Matt in spite of her parents' objections, and now she had to live with her decision. And he was probably also right that she didn't have a hope of being able to care for the two of them in the near future. And lastly, she concluded that she could not leave her son with her parents to raise when they resented her decisions.

That evening she collected their things and told her mother that she wouldn't be needing her for awhile, and left. Unable to work, she had quit her job. She didn't even bother to go out looking for another one. She couldn't even leave her son while she was looking and very few businesses would hire someone carrying a baby to the interview. Besides, she told herself, I don't have the skills to get a better job anyway.

She just laid around her apartment for another week until the money she had totally ran out. She was down to her last

$3 when she called the county aid department and asked what she had to do to apply for welfare for herself and her son.

"Just come down tomorrow between 9 and 4," the woman said in a gruff tone of voice. "And be sure you bring evidence of your child's birth too."

"How much will I be able to get?" Kia asked meekly. By this time she was entirely intimidated by the woman.

"How should I know?" the woman snapped. "Listen, if you want help, come in. If you don't, then don't come in." With that she hung up on Kia.

She just sat there for several minutes as the tears welled up inside. How did I get myself into such a mess? she asked herself. It seems like there is no one I can turn to for help. It was a sleepless night for Kia. She tossed and turned as her mind continued to go over her problems. But, having no other alternatives she could see, the next morning she got dressed and caught the bus downtown.

The welfare office was full of women with children waiting to talk with one of the counselors. Kia sat down next to a large woman trying to manage three busy children. Seeing the anguished look on Kia's face she said, "This your first time here, honey?"

Kia replied, "Yes, have you been here before?"

"Sure, honey," the affable woman replied, restraining the now screaming children. "I tried makin' it on my own but it just ain't no use. Every time I get a man he just ups and leaves. Welfare took my check away from me last time, so I'm just stayin' single." She looked at Kia and saw the tears in her eyes. "Listen, honey, it ain't so bad. They'll give you $600 a month with one child. And if you can pick up some side money you'll be OK. I ain't gettin' rich, but at least we ain't goin' hungry no more."

Six hundred a month! Kia thought to herself. That will hardly pay the rent and utilities. "I can't get by on $600 a month!" she blurted out.

"Well then, child, you better move to someplace where you can. Cause that's all you're gonna' get here."

A depressed and defeated Kia spent the majority of that day sitting and waiting, or talking to one social worker after another. "Have you tried to work?" one asked.

"Yes," was her reply, "but I couldn't make enough to live."

"Well, where was your last job? Did you make enough to qualify for unemployment? Do you have any family that will help? Do you have any savings? Are you pregnant now?" And on and on it went.

Finally, at the end of the day the last person she saw told her, "You'll be hearing from a social worker in the next couple of days to check on your living conditions. Do you have enough money for food?"

"Yes," she lied. By this time she was so frightened by the whole process she would have willingly left and forgotten the entire thing. She was made to feel like a beggar and her self-esteem was totally stripped away.

True to their word, the welfare system sent a social worker to interview Kia and then recommended that she receive temporary aid for dependent child care. By this time she was down to virtually no food in the apartment and was nearly a month behind on rent and utilities. So even when the first check arrived it took nearly all of it just to get the urgent bills caught up. Kia knew she was developing slothful habits, including sleeping late and watching television nearly all day long. She rarely went out except to shop for food. Even then she felt like a second-class citizen when she paid for the food with food stamps.

It was during one of these infrequent outings that she saw a sign posted on one of the grocery store windows that read: "Out of luck? Feel like nobody cares? Call the single parents' support group 555-5012." Kia thought about the notice all that day. She did feel like nobody cared whether she lived or died. Welfare helped her to survive, but only because she had a child to feed. Every month she could feel her self-esteem dropping lower as the bills piled up. Now she had to dodge the apartment manager because she was over a month late on her rent. She had received two notices from the utility company, and Christmas was coming: a prospect that thoroughly depressed her. She and her mother were constantly bickering over her accepting welfare.

"Nobody in our family has ever been a beggar," her mother shouted over the phone. But she offered no help to Kia in paying her bills. Later that afternoon Kia dressed her baby and went back to the grocery store where she had seen the notice. She jotted down the number and went looking for a phone. When she rang the number she heard, "Singles' support group, how may we help you?"

It was the first time in a long time that Kia had heard anyone address her cordially and pleasantly. She answered, "I'm not really sure. I saw your notice in the store window and decided to call. What do you do?"

On the other end of the line Sally Mulkey quickly and efficiently outlined the support group she had helped to form at her church, ending with, "What is your name?"

Hesitantly, Kia answered, "I'm Kia Boatman. I didn't know you were a part of a church group. I'm sorry for bothering you. I'm not a churchgoer."

Quickly, Sally responded, "Please don't hang up, Kia. We're here to help you if we can. You don't have to be a part of any church." She went on to describe her circumstances when she had first asked for help. "Just having someone who cared whether I lived or died really meant a lot to me," Sally said. "I decided to see if I could help others as I had been helped. That's how singles support got started. Could you come in, Kia? We would really like to help if we can."

"I'm sorry," Kia replied, "I don't have any transportation. I don't think I can."

"Well, I don't want to push you, Kia. But if you want to come I'll be glad to come over and pick you up."

"Why would you do that?" Kia asked, surprised by Sally's offer. "You don't even know me."

"Because you wouldn't have called unless you need help. I want you to know that someone *does* care. Would you like me to pick you up?"

"No, that won't be necessary," Kia replied. She didn't

know how to respond next. She was skeptical because of what she had heard about cult groups preying on desperate people.

After a couple moments of uncomfortable silence, Sally said, "I know you're wondering if we're some kind of weird group, Kia. All I can say is you're welcome to call the church office and check us out. Also, if you feel pressured, just take your time and call me if you want to talk."

"No," Kia replied desperately, "I *do* need help. Could I come by this afternoon?"

Kia was but one of dozens of single mothers helped by Sally and her team of volunteers that first year. Their procedures were honed over the months of counseling to where they could separate the singles into various categories of need. Almost all needed financial help, either temporary or long-term. Others needed immediate attention because of physical abuse or emotional problems. In reality Kia was fortunate. She had no overwhelming debts nor did she suffer from depression to the point of contemplating suicide.

She was first counseled by Sally to determine the extent of her problems and then it was recommended that she meet with a financial counselor, just as Sally herself had when she asked for help. Since Kia's financial problems consisted primarily of past-due rent and utilities, the counselor recommended to the head of the benevolence committee that the bills be brought current — which they did from reserve funds. Then Kia was referred to another vocational counselor to evaluate her potential job options.

After giving Kia some aptitude tests the counselor recommended that she be trained in word processing and data entry at one of the local technical schools.

"But how would I ever be able to pay for it?" Kia asked as the counselor outlined the recommendation. "And what would I do with the baby while I'm at school?"

"The committee has voted to pay for your training with a no-interest loan," the counselor said. "You can pay it back after you get a job that will meet your needs. Sally has arranged for some of the older women who have been helped by the singles group to baby-sit for you the three evenings that the classes meet."

"I don't know what to say," Kia said, almost crying. "You've done more to help me than anyone in my life."

"That's why the Lord put us here," the counselor responded. "Maybe someday you'll be able to help someone else, just as Sally is doing with you."

The counselor then went on to ask Kia about her spiritual life, knowing that she had grown up in a local church, but quite obviously without a personal relationship with Jesus Christ. As is often the case he had the privilege of leading Kia to the Lord, building on the foundation laid by Sally and her volunteers.

Kia completed the training course at the technical school and was eventually hired by a Christian businessman from the church. At first the finances were extremely tight and she required help from the benevolence fund on several occasions to pay car insurance premiums, to buy a small car from one of the other members, and to cover some medical expenses. After a year she was offered a job as a court recorder and trained by the county government. Within another year she was making nearly $30,000 a year!

Unfortunately, her husband remarried, thereby removing any hope of reconciliation. Two years later Kia married an attorney she met through her job. Both are Christians, serving in their own capacities. He is one of the church's referral advisors and Kia is a financial counselor and teaches a singles' financial workshop in the church.

A PRINCIPLE TO REMEMBER:
God often provides beyond the need level.

If you then, being evil, know how to give good gifts to your children, how much more shall your Father who is in heaven give what is good to those who ask Him!
(Matthew 7:11)

■ 4 THE FINANCIAL STRUGGLES OF A SINGLE PARENT

It would be great if all the situations facing single parents worked out as well as that of Sally, whom we met in the last chapter. Many times we like to think that when someone, such as Sally, commits her life to the Lord, He will miraculously intercede on her behalf and cure the problems. Unfortunately, it doesn't usually work out that way. God doesn't force His will on us and unless the divorcing spouse is willing to listen and obey God's direction, he or she will walk away from the marriage.

All too frequently a wayward spouse will even rationalize his or her actions on the basis of instruction from some misguided counselor, Christians included. In such circumstances it is difficult to do much more than comfort the grieving party and help where possible. Unless and until the spouse recognizes the error of his or her way, no amount of counseling will help. It often sounds like a cliché to say to someone whose mate has left and cannot be persuaded to return, "Pray about it and turn him (her) over to the Lord." But in reality, that is the prescription given in God's Word according to Philippians 4:6, "Be anxious for nothing, but in everything by prayer and supplication with thanksgiving let your requests be made known to God."

In most divorce situations both parties are actively seeking to get out of the marriage. In the heat of constant arguments and financial pressures divorce looks like a viable, even attractive, option. However, what frequently happens is the problems get worse for both parties once they separate. We have looked at a few examples of women whose marriages dissolved and their financial situations got worse, and that is the norm, not the exception. The same can be said of the husband's situation, to a lesser degree.

Sometimes the opposite is true. When the marriage dissolves the wife is able to generate a greater level of income and her situation appears to improve. We have probably all met one or two divorcees who remarried the "perfect" man and lived happily ever after. Unfortunately, it is too often this situation that is publicized and the impression given that it is the norm. It is not!

There are some fundamental principles that deal with the subject of marriage and divorce. In spite of what our "enlightened society" says, these have not changed. If I could accomplish one thing through this book, it would be to convince any couple that they are better off married than divorced if they're willing to work at it, regardless of what they feel, or have heard to the contrary.

God Hates Divorce

In our generation divorce claims nearly 50 percent of all first marriages. It is estimated that 40 percent of all church members have been divorced at least once. In light of this, one would logically think church leaders—pastors, deacons, elders, etc.—would make divorce the topic of most of their teaching. Instead the church has skillfully skirted the issue, lest they offend too many of the "flock."

It would be difficult to assemble a board of deacons or elders in most churches if the biblical admonition against a divorced person serving in these capacities were applied absolutely. Obviously the same could be said of other qualifications, such as the management of their children, the love of money, their reputation outside the church, and so on. But for the purposes of this book we'll limit the discussion to divorce.

How many sermons have you heard taught on the subject of divorce as a sin? Not many, I suspect, unless your pastor is an individual without fear of reprisal. It could be argued that to attack the topic of divorce is to open wounds in the lives of many people. That is true. But it would be a rare divorcee who would not counsel others not to get divorced. Those who have lived through the hurt and rejection of a divorce know from whence they speak. More often than not it's the unrepentant person who deliberately chose to abandon his or her commitment who is offended. In fact, they look to the church to approve and condone their actions many times. "After all," they say, "who could live like a Christian in that situation?"

Someone sent me a set of cassette tapes from a large fundamental church where one of the church leaders had taught a series called, "The Five Reasons Why Divorce Is Biblical." It was clear that this teacher himself was divorced and remarried. He was totally convinced in his own mind that God had told him to divorce his first wife because she was a hindrance to his "ministry." His new wife was obviously God's perfect mate for him.

Later I heard that this church had several staff who had gotten divorced while serving there. They obviously "felt" the calling of God to find their perfect mate also. Students in this church's Christian school were being exposed to the same material and I rather suspect will use it as justification to shop around until they find the perfect spouse. This teacher eventually became involved with several female students and was removed from his position, but not until a lot of damage had been done to impressionable young people.

Contrary to what any teacher today tells you, God *hates* divorce. "Every one who divorces his wife and marries another commits adultery; and he who marries one who is divorced from a husband commits adultery" (Luke 16:18). I find it difficult to read anything else into that passage. That doesn't mean divorce is the unpardonable sin, any more than other acts of disobedience. But to even hint that divorce is an acceptable cure for marital problems is akin to blasphemy. I understand the arguments used in conjunction with verses like Matthew 5:32, "But I say to you that everyone who divorces his wife, *except for the cause of unchastity,* makes her commit adultery; and whoever marries a divorced woman commits adultery." But in Matthew 19:6ff the Lord tells us: "Consequently they are no longer two, but one flesh. What therefore God has joined together, let no man separate."

Take it on the counsel of God's Word that if divorce is allowed for any reason it is only for immorality. And even so, there is no indication that divorce *must* be the alternative. It would depend on whether or not the offending party repents and asks for forgiveness.

A PRINCIPLE TO REMEMBER:
Vows are sacred promises not to be broken.

A poor, yet wise lad is better than an old and foolish king who no longer knows how to receive instruction. (Ecclesiastes 4:13)

You Can Make It Work

There are times in nearly every marriage where it seems barely tolerable. I know that was true in my marriage for the first several years. Judy and I came out of non-Christian backgrounds with little or no training in a good marriage relationship. Consequently we argued about nearly everything. My days were filled with work and school, while hers were filled with children. We found our free time to be incompatible. I wanted to study and then do nothing; she wanted to get out of the house and go someplace. These situations make for some big arguments and hurt feelings on both sides.

We live in a generation that has not been taught the importance of keeping vows. Today it is socially acceptable to file for bankruptcy with no concern for repaying the creditors who extended trust in the form of money. Certainly some people are forced into bankruptcy, but the vast majority choose it as a legal means to avoid an unpleasant situation. Often the lessons aren't learned and the symptoms reoccur time and time again.

Contract law is so detailed that the average couple has no concept of what they are signing. The most successful lawyers are those who can word an agreement so their client can escape without penalty, if necessary. Often the basic intent is not to ensure that both sides are fairly represented, but rather to provide a means of escape if circumstances change.

Unfortunately the same can also be said of marriage. The words *until death do us part* don't really have any significance to most couples. Marriage is entered into with the idea that if it doesn't work out, I can always get out. With that basic assumption in mind a marriage *will* seldom work out. There are just too many potential areas of conflict between two virtually independent people.

It is only when two people make an absolute commitment to each other that a marriage can function as God intended. It is unrealistic to think that conflicts won't occur. They will. But if a husband and wife know the other person is irrevocably committed to the marriage, the problems can be resolved. If, however, one spouse is always walking on eggshells for fear of his or her partner bailing out in a conflict, the stress will create even more conflict, and the situation will escalate beyond control.

Again . . . and Again . . . and Again

Perhaps my most unusual marriage counseling situation was with a couple who had been divorced and remarried (to each other) three times.

Jack and Marcia were married while he was a pilot in the Air Force. As is normal for military personnel, Jack was shipped around the world periodically and Marcia was left to oversee the packing of their things and then follow along later. She was a registered nurse and had been totally self-supporting for several years prior to their marriage. The frequent moves put a tremendous strain on their relationship, especially because Marcia could no longer work as a nurse except as a fill-in. They made an adequate amount of money but it was always tight financially. Since Marcia actually had more free money before they were married, it placed an even further strain on their marriage. Their first child was born shortly before Jack was due to be released from the service. What neither of them knew was that this child would be born with several abnormalities that would necessitate multiple operations.

Jack had already accepted a position with a major airline as a flight engineer. Contrary to popular opinion, new flight engineers aren't paid extremely well and with the loss of base housing and free medical care they actually netted less than they had made in the service.

The health problems with their child again necessitated that Marcia not work, except on a part-time basis. Since the airline's insurance excluded the preexisting medical condition of their child, they ended up with several thousands of dollars in medical bills.

They struggled through the first year in civilian life barely making it financially, while their communications level declined steadily. Then Jack was offered a chance to move up to copilot with another airline at a substantial increase in pay. Marcia naturally thought the increase would resolve their financial situation and allow her more free money to buy things like furniture, clothes, and a new car to replace her 10-year-old one.

What she hadn't counted on was how cheap Jack was when it came to spending money on creature comforts. He was a very security-conscious person who always thought in terms of long-range goals, the first of which was to save for their children's college education. When Marcia pointed out that they didn't have children, just a child, Jack reminded her that such thinking was typical of a woman's mentality. As you would imagine, the communications degraded from that point on. Despite Jack's vehement objections, Marcia accepted a full-time nursing position at a local hospital. She worked the third shift and during the times when Jack was traveling she hired a live-in baby-sitter.

The real battles began when Jack attempted to impose restrictions on how Marcia could spend her money. His priority was additional savings; hers was the purchase of creature comforts. After a particularly bitter argument one evening, and while Jack was gone on a trip, Marcia opened up her own checking account and applied for her own credit cards. She effectively separated her finances from those of her husband.

When Jack discovered what she had done, he was furious. We'll pick up the conversation there.

"Marcia, if you want to find yourself living alone, you're definitely on the right track," Jack said bitterly.

"Well, maybe I do," she responded just as bitterly. "You know, Jack, you're about as cheap a human being as ever walked the face of this earth. I'm tired of living like we don't have two pennies to rub together. If you won't buy the furniture we need, I will!"

"Oh no you won't," Jack threatened. "I'll throw that junk out in the street. I'm the head of this family and I decide what we buy or don't buy."

"You've got a lot to learn about what being a husband and father is all about," Marcia shouted in his face. "When you discover what it is, you call me. In the meantime Becky and I are moving out."

"Go ahead, see if you can make it on your own. You'll come begging for my help before a month is out."

"I wouldn't ask you for anything if our lives depended on it," she screamed. "I'd be afraid we might divert some of your precious money."

That evening Marcia moved into a motel room, and a few days later into an apartment near the hospital. The first few months were a struggle but then she was made shift supervisor at a substantial increase in pay, and things got easier. She felt like she loved Jack but knew they had irreconcilable differences. We're so opposite, we'll never be able to get along, she thought.

The next month Marcia filed for divorce. When Jack was served with the papers he was totally shocked. He knew, as she did, that they were having serious problems, but he never considered the reality of a divorce. To him it was just an idle threat he had used in the midst of anger.

After several attempts to dissuade Marcia from the divorce Jack realized it was hopeless. In the meantime Marcia found out that she was pregnant with their second child. She decided to say nothing to Jack and went through with the divorce. It soon became obvious that she was pregnant and Jack seemed to develop a totally different attitude toward her. He would always bring her small gifts, which was totally out of character for him. From time to time he even would buy a nice piece of antique furniture and give it to her. They saw more and more of each other and finally Jack proposed that they get remarried.

Marcia was hesitant at first because she had more freedom on her own as well as more spendable income, but gradually Jack won her over and she agreed.

They were remarried in a small, private ceremony and returned to their previous home. For a while things were different. Jack really tried to ask Marcia's counsel on what she felt they needed. He would even ask her opinion about a potential investment he was considering. She began keeping the checking account, but lacking Jack's bent for detail, she made several critical mistakes, including allowing the checkbook to go unbalanced for three months. Then one day Jack was bringing in the mail and noticed a letter from their bank marked, "Urgent information — respond immediately." Opening the letter he found a delinquent balance notice and overdraft charges amounting to nearly $50. He blew his stack.

"Marcia, what is this?" he shouted at her without warning.

"What is what, Jack?"

"These overdraft charges. Don't you keep the checkbook balanced?"

"I let it go a couple of months because I got busy with the new baby. But I know I should have enough money in our account."

"Well it's pretty obvious you don't," Jack fumed. "That's it, Marcia, I'm taking over the account again. You just don't have any common sense when it comes to money."

She started to put up an argument, but realized it was useless. Jack was back to his old habit of worrying about money all the time. She realized she should have been balancing the account and apologized, promising Jack she would do better from now on.

"Oh no you won't," Jack shouted as he threw down the paper he was reading. "I'll keep the checkbook from now on. You haven't got the brains to manage money."

Jack's caustic comments cut Marcia to the quick. In spite of her education and success as a nurse, she had always suffered from an inferiority complex. From that point on, their relationship continually deteriorated until a few months later Marcia decided to leave again. The one thing that made her life totally intolerable, she said, was that she felt Jack distrusted her to handle their money.

"It's like he is penny wise and pound foolish," Marcia share with her best friend, Laura, one afternoon a week before she decided to leave. "He resents it if I want to buy a couch or a chair, but then he'll go out and invest $10,000 in some new deal. I feel like I'm a slave in my own home."

"You don't need to put up with that," Laura told her. "I'd leave him if it were me. You can make it on your own. You're not a child. Don't let any man treat you like one."

The more Marcia thought about what Laura said, the madder she got. He is treating me like a child, she thought. I don't need this.

Two weeks later she and her daughters moved out. Six months later she and Jack were divorced again. This time Jack decided that he had had enough also and determined that he wouldn't even try to see Marcia again.

But as if often the case, the Lord had other ideas. Jack became ill with a stomach problem that required him to be hospitalized. While in the hospital he contracted a staph infection that became life threatening. Marcia heard about it through a mutual friend and came to visit him. Being a nurse she recognized the seriousness of his illness and ultimately stayed on to care for him when he left the hospital. It was her concern and care that probably saved Jack's life.

It took nearly a year for Jack to be restored to full health and flying status. During that period Marcia provided the majority of the income by working weekends at the hospital. Finances were extremely tight but Marcia proved her capabilities by managing all the finances and making ends meet. Often it required shopping at thrift stores and buying dented cans and day-old bread, but they made it.

Jack asked Marcia to remarry him near the end of that first year. She was reluctant to do so even though she realized that she loved him. "Jack, you have never allowed me to share your life before. You and I are different people but somehow you always felt that I had to fit into your idea of the perfect wife, which seems to be a nonperson. Do you really think you can share you life with anyone and allow them to be themselves?"

Jack's response was, "I've learned a lot about needing other people over this last year, especially you. I know I can. Will you marry me?"

Marcia said yes and they were remarried, again in a very quiet ceremony.

As Jack got back on his feet and resumed his career, many of the old habits returned. When they had virtually no money he was willing to accept Marcia's help, but now that he was making in excess of $100,000 a year again he took over the finances. Once more their lives became one argument after the other, always over money. Within two years of their second remarriage Jack left and filed for divorce.

This time it was Marcia who was convinced the marriage was over for good. She was emotionally drained of all feelings, or so it seemed to her at the time. Several times she said she seriously considered suicide. The only thing she felt had stopped her was her daughters' need for her. The first-born had become a timid, frightened child as a result of all the upheaval in her life. Marcia even had to withdraw her from school for a period of time because she would go into hysteria when left there.

Fortunately Jack was supporting them adequately this time, so work was an option for Marcia, not a necessity. She had relocated several states away from Jack, trying to get her own life back together.

Jack began to drink periodically, and then often. He was well on his way to becoming a "down time" alcoholic when by chance he was flying with a copilot, Andy Greer, who recognized that he had some real problems. Andy made it a point to maintain contact with Jack and often asked him to attend a meeting of the Fellowship of Christian Airline Personnel. This is an organization made up exclusively of airlines employees who meet monthly to share Christ.

Jack's usual response was, "I appreciate the offer, Andy, but religion just isn't for me. I don't have a need for a crutch."

"I can see that, Jack," Andy said with some intended sarcasm. "That's why you drink when you're not flying though, isn't it? You need to get away from reality."

Jack's emotions flared. "What I do is none of your business, or anyone else's. I do my job, and I'm good at it."

"I agree," Andy nodded. "You're an excellent pilot. And if that's all there was to life, you'd do great. But life goes on after flying, Jack, and one day we'll both be faced with the fact we can't fly anymore. Then what?"

For the next several weeks Andy continued to ask Jack to attend one of the meetings with him. He could see Jack's life slipping into a Jekyll-and-Hyde pattern—the efficient pilot and the drunken civilian. Finally Jack agreed to attend a meeting, simply to get Andy off his back.

At this particular meeting an ex-Air Force fighter pilot gave his testimony about how Christ had come into his life while a prisoner-of-war in Vietnam. He also shared how he and his wife had never been able to get along before because of their differences over money.

The more he talked, the more Jack saw his own life, altered only by the different circumstances. He went away from that meeting a changed man; not from the outside yet, but from the inside. He willingly attended several more of the meetings, where each time he felt the speaker was talking directly to him. By the fifth month Jack had become a regular attendee, had begun to actually read the Bible, and was asking Andy questions about Christianity every time he saw him. Finally Andy asked him, "Jack, would you like to have Jesus Christ as your Savior?"

Jack thought for several moments without responding. He had always known that something was missing in his life. No matter how much money he made, he was always fearful of the future. The more he tried to be a good husband, the more he fouled up his and Marcia's life. His drinking was becoming a daily problem now and even when he flew he found himself needing another drink. Suddenly he realized that it was God who had been calling him all these years. He just hadn't recognized the voice. "Yes I would, Andy," Jack said as he began to pour out his heart. "My life's a mess and I ruin everything I touch."

That day Andy led Jack to the Lord. Jack's conversion was one of those Damascus road experiences. He never had the desire to drink after that day. He joined a good church that Andy recommended, and, most important, began a consistent walk with the Lord.

He tried several times to call and talk to Marcia but she refused to speak with him. Then one evening, after an all-day trip, he decided to go see her. The next morning he was knocking on her door.

Marcia opened the door to see a red-eyed, rumpled pilot, still in his uniform standing in her doorway. She naturally assumed he was drinking and in some kind of trouble.

"What do you want?" she said curtly. "Jack, if you need help, go somewhere else, would you?"

"I don't need help, Marcia," he replied as he saw himself in the window next to the door. "I know I must look crummy but I haven't been drinking. In fact, I don't drink anymore. I just need to talk to you for a few minutes. After that I'll go if you want." Jack spent the next two hours sharing with Marcia what had happened in his life.

Clearly skeptical, she said, "Are you sure this isn't just another one of your side ventures, Jack? I thought things had changed last time, but we're so different and you want someone you can rule over. That won't be me."

"I know you have a perfect right to feel that way. All I ask is that you give me a chance to at least see you and the girls for awhile. I feel so totally different inside now. I believe I am a different person."

Something in what Marcia saw told her that Jack *was* different and she agreed to see him once a month on Sundays. This relationship continued for nearly a year, with their feelings for each other gradually being restored. In December of that year Jack asked Marcia to marry him once again. She agreed. Only this time they were remarried with a full ceremony. Jack decided that since he was a new man, this would be a new marriage.

Over the next year together Marcia did indeed see a new man in Jack. He still had some bad habits, but the difference was that he had a humble spirit and readily admitted his faults when he blew it. In a move totally out of character for him, he asked Marcia if she would be upset if he voluntarily took a demotion from pilot to copilot.

"Why in the world would you want to do that, Jack?" she asked. "Wouldn't that mean a cut in pay too?"

"Yes it would," he replied. "But I would really like to get more involved in winning others to Christ, and as a senior copilot I can choose my own schedule more than I can as a captain."

This so totally floored Marcia that she didn't really know what to say. She had seen changes in Jack over the year they had been remarried, but never one so totally out of character. She replied, "Whatever you want, that's what I want too, Jack." Marcia began to cry as Jack put his arms around her.

That day Jack had the privilege of leading his wife to the Lord, just as Andy had done for him earlier. These events occurred nearly 12 years ago now. Jack and Marcia are still married. They now have three children and Jack is an internationally known speaker for Christ. Marcia heads up the local right-to-life counsel in their community and writes for several Christian magazines on the emotional and psychological problems of abortion. Both she and Jack agree, the fourth time's a charm.

A PRINCIPLE TO REMEMBER
God is faithful, though every man fails.

Trust in the Lord with all your heart, and do not lean on your own understanding. In all your ways acknowledge Him, and He will make your paths straight.
(Proverbs 3:5-6)

■ 5 HOUSING, CARS, AND KIDS

The three big expenses in any divorced parent's budget are housing, cars, and kids, in that order. As the kids get older, the order shifts to put them first. But in the early years most divorcees struggle to find adequate housing they can afford. A little later in this book I offer some budget advice that will help most single parents. But for right now we need to address these three budget busters.

Housing

The average American family (making approximately $25,000 a year) will spend about 35 to 40 percent of their net income (after taxes and giving) on housing. This amount, about $650 per month, seems inadequate in many parts of the country. But when compared to the $350 to $400 that most divorcees have to spend it seems like an impossible dream. Most single parents know the frustration of looking for an apartment, much less a home, where the total monthly expenses (rent, utilities, telephone, etc.) must be $400 or less. Ultimately many single parents migrate to run-down neighborhoods where the crime rate is high, but the rents are low.

Brittany was one such parent. She was recently divorced after four years of marriage and had one child. Her ex-husband was a drug user and dealer who had been arrested and sent to prison shortly after their divorce. Brittany worked as a typist in the local county's tax office with an annual salary of $13,000. She had become a Christian through a ministry that evangelized door-to-door. She regularly attended a small independent church where she was well supported spiritually. But since many of the other members were also single parents, many in more need than her, she realized that she could not expect much financial help from the church. In fact, Brittany herself often gave to the needs of some of the other singles in the group.

While married, their finances had cycled from almost nothing to thousands a month, as her husband bought and sold drugs. She guessed what he was doing and confronted him several times. Each time he denied it, claiming that the money came from winning bets at his work. Finally, when she realized he was on drugs himself, she knew he must be dealing in them and begged him to get help. He categorically denied any involvement in drugs, even when she found several stashes of drugs around their apartment. People began coming to their door late at night and her husband would sell them drugs and take the money. Twice he was accosted at gunpoint and even she and the baby had been threatened by a drug addict. Finally she left and relocated in a small apartment. She felt fortunate to secure the job with the county since it also provided health insurance.

Shortly after she filed for divorce her husband was arrested, and within six months was convicted, sentenced, and shipped off to prison. Brittany quickly found that her income would only cover the bare necessities and the $475-a-month rent was beyond her meager salary. She went shopping for an apartment within her budget and was quickly discouraged. The only thing close was a run-down apartment in the center of the known drug district. She refused to locate in this area and realized that something had to happen or she would eventually be forced out of where she was.

She discussed her problems with her singles' support group that met Wednesday evenings in different homes. We join them there.

"You know, I'm willing to work more, if I could," Brittany said to the group of six women and a man who met that evening. "But by the time I hire a baby-sitter I'd be lucky just to break even. Besides, who would I find to keep my little girl in the evenings?"

"I don't believe God wants you to abandon your daughter," one of the other women said. "You wouldn't see her except on weekends."

"I know it," Brittany said as the tears came. "It's already hard enough. Last week my little girl started calling her baby-sitter 'Mommy.' It almost broke my heart. The first words she said were to a stranger, instead of her mother."

"You can always go on welfare and get ADC," one of the

women said. "At least that way you can stay home with your kid."

"Yeah, how much does that pay though?" another woman said in a disgusted tone. "Maybe $600 a month. So you get to stay home with your kids and beat the rats off too. No thanks, I want somethin' more out of life than being a government ward. I've lived in those welfare houses before. I'll work three jobs before I'll do that again."

The discussion lasted for the better part of 30 minutes before another woman, Maye, spoke up. "You know, we're totally ignoring the basic principle that God provides for our needs. Maybe that's why He has us here tonight. We all share similar problems, right?"

"Right!" answered everyone.

"Brittany, I'm having the same kinds of problems you are. My money just won't stretch far enough to cover all my living expenses, and my ex-husband pays his child support every month. But if we pooled our resources together, we'd have enough money to meet both our needs."

"How could we do that?" Brittany asked.

"By renting an apartment large enough for both of our families and sharing expenses. I'd like to go to school in the evenings and learn about computers, but I can't afford a baby-sitter either. If you could watch my daughter a couple of nights, I'd be glad to do the same for you, if you need it."

"Hey, that's not a half bad idea," one of the other women said enthusiastically. "What about that, Brit?"

"I'll have to give it some thought," Brittany said as she considered the idea. "What if we don't get along though?"

"If we can't make it work as Christians, then we have a fundamental problem with the Lord's Word, I'd say," Maye replied. "Besides, what do we have to lose? Do you have any better idea?"

Brittany had to admit that she didn't have any other viable ideas. By the next week she had decided to give it a try, and within another week had located a three-bedroom apartment that was only slightly more than her present apartment. The next month she and Maye moved in.

The first few weeks were a real adjustment for the two families as they went through the normal territorial disputes of who got the shower when, and who cleaned up the dishes when. But within a month they had worked out a plan that assigned jobs to each in turn, and things were progressing relatively smoothly.

All the expenses were split down the middle and they even found that they could share rides together, except on Maye's school nights. By merging the two incomes they had effectively created a family situation with slightly more than an average income available. All the bills were paid and each was able to begin building a small savings.

Brittany found one of the available solutions to housing costs for single parents: to combine their buying power and pool resources. Unfortunately, too often our independent spirits as Americans keep us from doing that. We don't want the bother of merging our lives with someone else's because of the inconvenience. A look at some of the immigrants from other countries to the U.S. is an enlightening experience. They will usually combine two or more families' incomes in one home to conserve expenses. Each family makes the sacrifices necessary to achieve their long-range goals: to own their own businesses eventually. As Solomon said in Ecclesiastes 4:9-10, "Two are better than one because they have a good return for their labor. For if either of them falls, the one will lift up his companion. But woe to the one who falls when there is not another to lift him up."

There are other housing options available to the single parent who is willing and able to work—and use some ingenuity. I wish I could take credit for many of the ideas I have shared with single mothers over the years, but in honesty most of them I learned from another single parent who had found a solution to her (or his) dilemma.

Eileen was a 40-year-old mother of three children who ranged in ages from 6 to 18. Her husband, a deacon in their church, had run off with his 30-year-old secretary, a mother of four herself. When he left, he also cleaned out their savings account, leaving Eileen with $300 dollars to her name.

Fortunately several members of her church rallied around her to help pay the bills that were coming due. Her job as an administrative assistant to a school superintendent would provide only about half of the current expenses in their home.

Shortly after her husband left, Eileen received a call from the mortgage company informing her that the house payments were two months in arrears and if they were not paid immediately, the lender would begin foreclosure proceedings. A friend from her church checked on the mortgage for her and discovered that Eileen's husband had taken out second and third mortgages to put money into his failing business, forging her name both times.

Suddenly, within a month she was faced with expenses that were double her income, a home going into foreclosure, and mortgages that totaled more than the value of the home. Needless to say, she was in a state of shock.

On the advice of an attorney from her church, she contacted the mortgage company vice president, told him the details of her situation, and offered to sign a voluntary foreclosure to save them the legal costs of evicting her family. The loan officer was sympathetic, but could do nothing to delay the legal action prescribed by his company. He did, however, arrange for Eileen to stay in the home for another month by paying rent equivalent to the total monthly mortgages. Since this sum was the equivalent of her total income, it was obvious something else would have to be worked out.

As she began the search for a place to live, it became obvious that even an apartment sufficient for a family of four would be too expensive on her salary. She was willing to rent a two-bedroom apartment or home but most landlords wouldn't agree to do so. Finally she found one who would and she rented a two-bedroom apartment for $500 a month. This took almost 50 percent of her take-home pay. After tithing to her church and paying the note on her car, it left her slightly more than $300 a month for everything else. Her 18-year-old daughter, Jamie, worked afternoons and weekends while attending the local junior college but could barely pay for her clothes, food, and transportation out of her part-time income in a fast-food restaurant.

Eileen realized that her friends from church wouldn't be able to support her deficit for any long period of time. As with most Americans, Christians included, most lived on what they made and it was their normal giving to the church that had been diverted to Eileen's need.

Jamie came to her one evening and said, "Mom, I can't let you carry this burden alone. I'm going to drop out of school and get a full-time job so I can help."

"What would you do, honey?" Eileen said as she hugged her daughter. "Work in a hamburger place? No, you stay in school. God has an answer; He always does. We just don't know what it is yet."

"But Mom, I don't mind, really. I can always go back later, when things get better."

"If the Lord wants you to be a chemist, you have to go to college. If you drop out you may never have the chance to go back. No, we'll wait a while and at least give God a chance to show us His way."

"Why do you think God let Daddy do what he did to us, Mom?" her daughter asked as they hugged each other.

"I don't believe God had any part in what your father did. He made his own choices and turned his back on the Lord. He will have to account for it one day. If not in this life, then in the next. We can't let something we can't change make us bitter. Then the enemy would have two victories."

Eileen struggled on for another two months, barely staying even with the help of friends. Then one evening when she went to pay her next month's rent, something happened that would alter her circumstances significantly.

Instead of finding the complex resident manager in his office, there was a new face. Eileen asked, "Where is Mr. Newton?"

"He doesn't work here anymore," replied the pleasant woman in a business suit. "I had to let him go."

"Oh," Eileen replied, not wanting to appear too nosey. "Well, I came to pay my rent. Can I pay you?"

"Yes," the woman answered. "I manage this complex as well as 12 others."

"Thirteen apartment complexes! That must keep you busy. How do you have time to collect rents?"

"I don't. But it's really hard to keep apartment managers. Mr. Newton was a nice enough man but he didn't keep good records, and apparently didn't maintain the complex very well according to the complaints I have received."

"I've only been in an apartment for three months so I don't really know. I do know I tried to get someone to fix our leaky faucets, but nobody has come as of yet."

"Several tenants have had similar complaints. This month alone we had three families move out because their apartments had problems that hadn't been handled for months. If you know of someone looking for a job as an apartment manager, I'd appreciate it if you would give them my card," she said as she handed one to Eileen.

"What is involved with being an apartment manager?" Eileen asked out of curiosity.

"It primarily involves collecting rents and scheduling maintenance on the apartments as tenants find problems. It also requires scheduling cleanup crews when someone vacates and acting as a rental agent for the company when apartments are available. Are you interested?"

"I don't think so," Eileen replied, slipping the card in her pocket. "I have a good job as the county school superintendent's assistant and I can't afford to leave it right now."

"You wouldn't have to," the manager said. "The job can normally be done in the evenings and weekends. It's really not a full-time position."

"Oh," Eileen said with new interest. "What does it pay?"

"We provide an apartment and all utilities, plus mileage if you have to use your car."

"I'm not sure I would be qualified. I've never even lived in an apartment until recently."

"I'd really rather train my managers myself," the manager said in response. "All I need is someone who is honest and willing to learn."

"That I am," Eileen said enthusiastically. "And I am very good at scheduling. I handle the scheduling of all the maintenance crews for the county school system now, and thoroughly enjoy it.'"

"It sounds as if you could handle the job then. Why don't you come by my office tomorrow and fill out an application. I'll need to run a background check on you, but that's routine."

"I'll be by tomorrow after work. Would 4:30 be acceptable?"

"That will be fine. I'll be looking for you."

The next day Eileen filled out the application for apartment manager. She was hired three days later and she and her family moved into a four-bedroom apartment, with all expenses paid. She turned out to be the best apartment manager the company had and often helped to train other new managers.

Her husband eventually filed for divorce in Texas where he relocated with the other woman who also divorced her husband. That marriage lasted less than two years until she ran off with still another man.

Another idea that single parents have found to help their living expenses is to become live-in companions. There are many elderly people throughout our society who would like to be able to remain in their own homes, rather than go to a retirement home or live with their children. Most would be able to if they had someone living with them who could keep the home cleaned, cook some meals for them, and help them with periodic transportation. Several single parents I have known had their housing needs met in this manner. They're a help to the elderly, in return for living in their home.

The obvious potential for conflict requires that both parties be compatible and honest upfront. Sometimes this arrangement doesn't work because of a clash of personalities, but very often it does, with all parties benefiting. Not the least are the children who benefit from the association with an older person. If children are to learn respect for the elderly in our society, they must be in close association with them.

A PRINCIPLE TO REMEMBER:
God gives a surplus to one, a lack to another.

Two are better than one because they have a good return for
their labor.
(Ecclesiastes 4:9)

Terrible Transportation

In our mobile society an automobile is no longer a luxury.
Except in large metropolitan areas where public transportation is available, it is a necessity. The cost of maintaining and
operating a car is enormous for the majority of us. For a
single parent living on a less than adequate income, that cost
is a budget buster.

The constant fear of the car breaking down, and the helpless feeling when it does, often tempts the single mother to
purchase a new car. Attracted by rebates and a low interest
rate, many single parents will finance a new car that will
totally wreck their budget. The average family will spend
about 15 to 18 percent of their disposable income buying a
medium-priced new car. The single parent, making slightly
more than half the income of the average family, will spend
upward of 25 to 30 percent. If she does, there is virtually no
way her budget will ever balance. A common plea among
single parents who ask for help is, "How can I get rid of this
car I bought, when it's not worth what I still owe on it?"

They end up selling the car at a loss, then paying the
balance on a car they don't even own anymore. And what's
worse, they don't even have their original car because they
used it as a trade-in on the new one.

No matter what happens to your old car, it is almost always
cheaper to repair the one you own than it is to purchase a
new one. You should never commit more than 15 to 16 percent of your disposable income to transportation. This percentage includes payments, maintenance, gasoline, insurance,
and so on. So before you buy a new car, just calculate your

net spendable income (after tithes and taxes), multiply it by .16, and that is the total your budget can handle. For a single parent making $18,000 per year the average net per month is $1,125. Thus the total amount that can be allocated to transportation is approximately $180 per month. A new car simply doesn't compute for most people. If, like Eileen, you have no expenses for housing or some other category of your budget, then you may be able to allocate more for transportation.

What are your alternatives? If you find that you must replace an older car, just remember that a good used car is significantly less expensive than a new one. If you want to calculate the loss in a new car after one year, a good rule of thumb is one-half of the original sticker price. That's a lot of depreciation when you consider it's probably half of the average single parent's income for a year!

The first logical alternative is to keep your old car going for as long as possible. Two factors usually work against the single parent trying to maintain an older car. First is the difficulty of locating a reliable, honest garage with a mechanic who can repair a modern car once it breaks down. Second is the fact that most single women don't have the funds to keep their cars in good repair anyway and they allow them to deteriorate until several major breakdowns occur within a short period of time. This would be discouraging to anyone, but to a single mom it becomes a nightmare. Often by this time she is facing a several hundred dollar repair bill on a car that is probably worth less than the total cost of repairs.

I can almost hear some of the single parents reading this book saying, "Well, you hit the problem right on the head. But what can we do about it?" Individually there is not a lot you can do about it. But collectively we can help solve the problem. A good friend whom I'll call Terry shared a similar situation that happened in his church.

The pastor of Terry's church was counseling with several of the divorced mothers in his congregation and the transportation problem kept recurring so regularly that he felt the church had to do something to help. One solution was to help with the cost of their car repairs, and he often did so out of his own funds. But in a few months he realized this was just dealing with the symptom, not the real problem. By the time the women came for help, their cars had virtually disintegrated from lack of maintenance, and the repair costs were overwhelming. For instance, usually these women had driven their cars on bad brakes long after the initial scraping sounds were first heard, sometimes until the car would no longer stop! By then the rotors or brake drums were badly scored and required replacing. So what might have initially been a $50 to $70 expense was now a $300 repair job!

After praying about the problem with his staff, the pastor suggested calling Terry and asking his opinion. Terry owned a large home building firm and was known to have a good working knowledge of car maintenance. He regularly restored old cars as a hobby and had become the resident counselor on car problems in the church.

"Terry, this is Lee. I really need your advice on something. Could we have lunch on Tuesday?"

"Sure, Lee. Tuesday's fine. I'll pick you up." Terry knew the pastor well enough to realize that when he called asking for help, it was usually a major problem.

The next Tuesday Terry and Lee Ennis met for lunch and the pastor outlined the problem.

"The difficulty is, by the time we get a chance to see these women, the problems are already out of hand. We would like to help if possible. Any ideas?"

"Not right off hand, Lee. But give me a couple of days to think about it. Maybe the Lord will give me an idea."

After the luncheon Terry did a lot of thinking and praying about the problem. He discussed it with his wife that evening at dinner.

"Why don't we have the same problems with our cars that single mothers do?" his wife, Karen, asked after he outlined what he and the pastor discussed.

"Well we do," Terry said as he thought about it. "Everybody does if they have a car with over 20,000 miles on it. But I either fix the problems myself or put the car right in the shop and have it fixed before it gets any worse."

"Why don't single mothers do the same thing then?" Karen suggested.

"Because they either don't recognize the problem or they don't know where to take it," Terry replied as he thought back to his conversation with Pastor Ennis. "Or they don't have the money to get it repaired."

"Well you know a lot about cars, Terry. Why don't you just have them call you when they think they have a problem. That's what I do."

"I couldn't handle all the calls I would probably get," Terry said hastily. "I would never get any work done."

"Then why don't you schedule a time when you would be willing to help them?"

"I wouldn't be able to see all of them even if I set aside a day a week."

"Maybe there are some other men in the church who would be willing to help," Karen suggested in her matter-of-fact manner. "Why not try it?"

The more Terry thought about Karen's suggestion, the more he decided it had some merit. The next day he called Pastor Ennis and explained his plan.

"Lee, I'll mention the idea at our men's prayer breakfast this week. You tell the single women that you and your staff are counseling that they can have a free car checkup the first Saturday of each month in the church parking lot. Just have them sign up with your secretary and then let me know how many will be coming."

"Great idea, Terry. I'll get right on it," Lee said. He felt like a weight had been lifted off his shoulders.

The first Saturday three single mothers showed up to have their cars checked. Two of the vehicles had major problems that needed immediate work. Terry arranged with the garage to do the work and bill the women at whatever their counselor said they could afford. What they didn't know was that Terry paid the difference himself.

As the word spread in the church, more women asked for help with their cars until Terry could no longer handle the load himself. By that time he had two other men who had volunteered to help. To limit the work they had to do, each woman was required to see a church counselor for a referral.

By the fourth month Terry had six volunteers working on alternate Saturdays. They would not only check out the cars but do minor maintenance such as oil changes, brake repairs, and tune-ups, to the extent their expertise allowed.

As the word spread outside the church through women sharing at work and other places, the church became like a magnet for single parents. Soon it was obvious to Terry that this could be a real area of ministry, both to the singles in his church and also to many unsaved women who desperately needed help. He had another idea:

"I would like to propose that we buy the gas station over on Main Street that went out of business and convert it into a car repair shop," Terry shared at the volunteer staff's Monday morning meeting. "We could hire a mechanic to do minor repairs full-time and help check out the cars on Saturdays, like we have been doing. I also suggest that we charge whatever the counselor says these women can afford and subsidize the difference through our benevolence fund."

"Won't that get to be pretty expensive?" one of the other volunteers asked.

"If we have the entire men's group behind it, the total cost would be less than $50 a month each. As the word gets out, I believe we'll have some others who would help also," Terry said as he sat back down.

After deliberating the idea for a few minutes, the men prayed about it and then voted unanimously to adopt the car repair center as a group project.

The church now has nearly 200 singles signed up for the car helps ministry, many of whom became Christians as a result of one man's commitment to help solve a problem.

Unfortunately this option is not available to most single parents, so they have to use other ideas. One idea available to most people is to buy a used car rather than a new one. The objection that many single women have to buying a used car is that they don't know how to tell a good one from a bad one. In reality, the same problem exists when buying a new car too. Remember that all those used cars were once new. So the lemons were out there from the beginning, only at a higher price. Here are some steps you can take to lessen the risk when buying a used car:

1. *Get help.* Almost always there are men (and women) within a church who have a very good understanding of automobiles. I have found that most people are glad to help another person evaluate a potential car, once they have narrowed down the search a little. Don't be hesitant to ask for help. The only way these people can exercise the gifts and abilities God has given them is for others to ask.

2. *Check it out.* The one thing you can count on is that a poorly made new car doesn't get better with age. Magazines such as *Consumer Reports* evaluate all new automobiles. If, for instance, you are considering a two-year-old Oldsmobile 88, go to the library and check a copy of the magazine in the year the car was originally sold. If it was graded a poor car when it was new, avoid it. It may be cheaper, but it may cost more in the long run.

3. *Check the warranty.* Many used cars carry a transferable warranty that may be good for up to 50,000 miles or more. If you have a concern about the potential cost of maintenance, these warranties usually cover the major power train items, which are the most expensive to repair. If you have a question about what the warranty will or will not cover, call the manufacturer.

Sometimes a dealer will offer a dealership extended warranty on a car he is selling. Be sure you have someone who knows contracts check it out very carefully. My personal experience has been that they exclude more than they cover.

The Best Sources for Used Cars

In talking with many people who buy and sell cars, I have found some common points of agreement in locating the best buys for the money. These certainly are not absolutes but they are a reliable guide when looking for a good used automobile:

1. *Check with friends and family first.* Often you will be

able to locate the best value by asking around your church to see if anyone has a dependable car for sale. Most people are basically honest and will tell you the truth about their car. This is particularly important if the car has more than 30,000 miles on it.

A second benefit is that sometimes they will self-finance all or a portion of the cost, which saves a great deal on interest. And in most states the sale of a private individual's car is not subject to sales taxes, which again translates into savings for you.

2. *Shop the local paper.* If you are unable to locate the right car through friends or family, the next best source is your local newspaper. Often people who buy a new car will elect to sell their used car themselves. As I said before, most people are basically honest and will tell you the real condition of their car, if you ask them the right questions, such as: Has it ever been in an accident? Has it been a low or a high maintenance car? Have teenagers driven it regularly? Did you buy it new? (I would rarely buy a second- or third-owner car.) How often has the oil been changed?

3. *Visit dealerships.* This is the most common source that used car buyers frequent because dealers are easily available, they arrange financing, and always have a supply of cars available. Remember that they also must mark up their cars to make a profit so, unless you know the owner by reputation, they may not always be as truthful as other sources.

4. *Try a wholesaler.* Wholesalers are car auctions where used cars are regularly sold. But unless you know a great deal about cars, I would suggest that you stay away from wholesale auctions. The low prices tend to attract many non-professional buyers, but they are often unpleasantly surprised. While some very nice cars pass through auctions, they are also places where dealers dump their worst cars. You may be buying the proverbial "pig in a poke."

A PRINCIPLE TO REMEMBER:
Ask for help when you have a need.

Without consultation, plans are frustrated, but with many counselors they succeed.
(Proverbs 15:22)

Child Care Costs

When our children were young, my wife Judy had the option to work at home or in an office. She opted to work at home until our youngest went off to college. That is an option virtually no single, divorced parent has in this generation. Unless they are willing to live on "aid to dependent children" at less than poverty income, they must work, usually outside the home.

I have heard all the arguments for and against single mothers working, especially those with small children. I can honestly say I don't know how they cope. Even with both husband and wife sharing the burden, it is difficult. But a working single mother with small children lives in a state of near emotional and physical exhaustion, unless she has some unusual circumstances.

Combine this with the financial pressures of child care and it is easy to see why many divorcees jump into a second marriage that they often regret. It's called desperation.

The cost of child care won't compute in the average family's budget. On an income of $24,000 a year, daily child care consumes nearly 13 percent of disposable income (about $2,100 to $2,400 per year). That amount simply cannot be worked into the normal family's budget and still leave funds for vacations, entertainment, eating out, etc. But since the child care is a by-product of the working wife, they have her income to do these things. So in reality she ends up working to support the child care center and family activities that are necessitated because of the pressures created by a working mother. As a counselor I realize it's not really that simple, but it often seems that way to me when couples outline their problems.

If the cost of child care won't compute in the average family's budget, it certainly won't compute in a single parent's more limited budget. Unfortunately it must! Child care for one preschooler runs about $150 per month in most parts of the country (higher in metro areas). For two children (the norm in most single parent families), it runs about $250 per month. That equates to about 15 to 22 percent of a single mother's disposable income. Is it any wonder why we have so many "latchkey" kids in America? As soon as the child is old enough to know not to burn the house down while he's home alone, he's on his own.

Adding to the guilt of parking a child in a daycare center, or in a private home, is the knowledge that most of them are being fed a constant diet of sex and violence through the television several hours each day. It's no wonder that we're having drug, sex, and suicide problems with our young generation. By the time most of them are in their early teens they have had more adult experiences than an average 30-year-old of two generations ago.

It's easy to put a guilt trip on single parents because they spend so little time with their children. Single parents love their children just as much as the average couple does. But what are the alternatives available to them? In reality, very few — without help from outside. The resources *are* available to solve this problem, but they are not in the hands of single parents. They are within the churches of America.

Unfortunately, as of this writing, the churches of America have not taken the lead in helping to solve the dilemma. As a result, the federal government has stepped in with a child care program that will increase taxes and still not solve the problem. It amazes me that taxpayers can be tricked into believing that the government can take a bad system and make it a winner by pouring more money into it. An education system that can't teach a child how to read and write in 12 years of study says it needs the children at a younger age to do the job. A welfare system that consumes over 80 percent of allocated funds in administrative overhead thinks it can administer child care centers better than private individuals. The cost to the single parents will go down, but the cost to the taxpayers will escalate out of control.

I don't fault the single parents for wanting the child care legislation—they need help. It's the church in America that has failed in its responsibility to help the poor among us. As a result many more Americans now look to the government as their source of aid, rather than looking to God. The solution is available; all it takes is caring Christians.

A few years back I met a single parent I'll call Pam, who has made a difference in her church in the area of child care for working singles. Pam had been a Christian for nearly three years when her husband, Cal, decided he had had enough of "religion" and told her he wanted a divorce.

"I just don't want to live with a religious fanatic," Cal said in response to Pam's question about why he wanted a divorce.

"But have I tried to force Christianity on you?" Pam asked as she tried to cope with Cal's attitude.

"Maybe not, but you sit around reading that stupid Bible all the time. I want to have some fun in life. I don't want to live with some saint."

"But Cal, I'm not trying to be a saint," Pam protested. "I didn't know my Bible study bothered you. I would be glad to do it when you're not here if it offends you."

"No, that's just a part of it, Pam. We have different friends now. I don't feel like bringing my friends over here because they don't go to church either. And I know you're not going drinking with us anymore."

"I don't have the desire to drink anymore, Cal. But that doesn't mean I don't love you. It's just that Jesus Christ is the center of my life now and I don't need to drink."

"See what I mean?" Cal shouted as he stormed out of the room. "You don't need to drink! Well neither do I! I do it because I like to!"

This scene was repeated often over the next several months until ultimately Cal packed up and left. He provided Pam with about $500 a month, obviously inadequate for her needs with three children from ages 3 to 12.

Pam began a search for a job that would at least meet her minimum needs. She ended up as a clerk for an insurance company, making about $1,000 a month. With two children in school she had only the three-year-old son to place in daycare. But as she shopped for a good daycare center she quickly found that the average fee of $150 a month was still pushing her budget to the limit. For her older two it meant that the 12-year-old became the baby-sitter for nearly two hours a day, until Pam returned home – often to find a raging war of wills going on between the two girls. She could see summer break coming and had no idea how she would handle that situation.

In the meantime Cal filed for divorce and was granted it on the grounds of incompatibility. The judge assigned child support of $375 a month. Suddenly Pam found herself in a deficit financially each month as the expenses exceeded her income. She made the necessary adjustments, which included eliminating any clothing budget, car maintenance, or eating out. Still her budget was tight, and she knew it was just a matter of time until it collapsed.

In the meantime she was having to deal with an entirely new problem. Her pastor called and asked if she would come by his office. She agreed and set up an appointment for that Friday.

Pam pondered all week what he might want of her. Perhaps he wants to know if we have any needs, she thought. Hers was a caring church that ministered to some of the poor in their community. When she arrived at the church office the secretary showed her into the pastor's study. Already there was another couple, whom Pam knew to be deacons in the church.

The pastor said, "Pam, I hope you'll take this the right way, but the church has decided to suspend your membership."

"What! But why?" Pam nearly shouted in her shock.

"Because we believe that divorce is a sin. Therefore you're living in sin and cannot hold your membership."

"But I didn't divorce my husband," Pam protested. "He divorced me. I wouldn't even agree to the divorce. But in this state either spouse can get a divorce if the judge agrees."

"That may be," the woman deacon said curtly. "But we also understand you have been sharing what happened with your Sunday School class. Is that right?"

"Well, yes," Pam admitted. "But I wasn't encouraging anyone else to get a divorce. I was sharing how difficult it is to be a single parent in our society."

"If you were truly innocent, you wouldn't be having financial problems," the pastor commented. "It is our belief that God is using this because you have hidden sins in your life."

"And we don't want to give others the idea that they can get divorced with no consequences," the woman added.

"You can still attend the church, Pam. But you won't be able to take communion or vote in church matters," the pastor said, looking at the floor.

"And you won't be allowed to speak up in Sunday School," said the deaconess. "You need to accept this as God's judgment, Pam, and repent of whatever is wrong in your life."

Pam sat there so stunned that she couldn't even defend herself. As the tears welled up in her eyes she stood up and walked out of the room. On her way home she got more and more angry. All kinds of thoughts crossed her mind, from suing the church to addressing the next Sunday service. But as she calmed down a bit she realized that neither was according to God's Word. I just won't allow them to drag me down to their pious level, Pam decided resolutely. The next Sunday she went out looking for a new church home.

Within a few weeks she had found a church in which she felt very comfortable, and she and the children were attending regularly. One evening her doorbell rang and when she opened the door, it was the pastor of the new church.

He introduced himself. "I'm Pastor Ross. I know you and your family have been attending our church, and I just wanted to drop by and welcome you."

Pam thanked him and then told him about her recent divorce and asked about the church's policy toward divorcees joining the church.

"We're a church made up of forgiven sinners," the pastor said. "If you know the Lord, that's our only requirement. We do require that all prospective members attend an orientation class before joining, but that is only to ensure that they all understand the plan of salvation first."

Pam joined the church and got involved in their singles' ministry. Some months later, at one of the evening meetings the subject of child care came up. Several of the single parents shared their dilemma of inadequate care for their children and their concern over the influence their children received at a secular facility. Several commented about the rock music that was played all day long. One woman shared that at one center the attendant watched pornographic videos during nap times. She learned about it from her three-year-old who uttered a few choice four-letter words.

Over the next several meetings an idea jelled. Why doesn't the church sponsor a daycare center for members that would be staffed by one full-time person and volunteers? It was agreed that the idea would be presented to the pastor.

Pastor Ross agreed wholeheartedly, and the child care center was born. Within six months all the necessary support had been raised through the singles' group, the necessary permits were obtained, and Pam had organized 12 women to assist the director who had been hired from a local facility.

The daycare center struggled along on limited funds for several months. Many of the mothers who applied for their children to attend were turned away, including Pam, because of the lack of resources. Just when it seemed that the idea would fall apart, Pam received a call one evening from a member who owned a large contracting firm in the city.

"Pam, I heard about your efforts to start a child care center at the church. The pastor said that it appears you'll have to shut it down. Is that right?"

"It would appear so," Pam said as she took a deep breath. She had not even admitted that inevitable prospect to herself. But the truth was they had not been able to pay the director her full salary for nearly two months now. The single parents just couldn't pay enough to get the center established.

"I understand some of the problems that single mothers are facing," he said. "My own daughter is in that same situation, and if it weren't for our help each month, she couldn't make it. Her husband has taken off and nobody knows where he is."

I know the feeling, Pam thought to herself. Half the women in our group don't get any support from their husbands.

"I would like to help, if it's OK," the man said. "I would like to make an anonymous gift to the center for the next couple of years."

"That would really help," Pam responded, not having any idea if he was talking about a gift of $100 or $1,000.

Two days later the pastor called to tell her that the gift to the center had arrived by mail. It was for $50,000! Over the next two years the church daycare center for single parents expanded to take care of nearly 60 children, including a summer program for "latchkey" kids. The program still functions on a can-pay basis, with all participants required to attend counseling sessions in the church. Most of the volunteer help now comes from mothers with husbands who want to help the single parents and from older members who have free time available. The church has also organized a "big brothers" association to help the children of single mothers have a male influence in their lives. They organize field trips, fishing and hiking outings, and a variety of other activities that most of these kids would otherwise miss out on.

All it takes is the commitment of one individual to marshal the troops that God has already equipped. Pam was willing to be used to help solve a problem that she faced.

A PRINCIPLE TO REMEMBER:
Don't judge others: Help.

For the whole Law is fulfilled in one word, in the statement, "You shall love your neighbor as yourself." But if you bite and devour one another, take care lest you be consumed by one another.
(Galatians 5:14-15)

■ 6 ALIMONY, CHILD SUPPORT, AND LAWSUITS

Any divorcee is faced with some difficult decisions:

- Should I ask for alimony?
- Should I keep the home?
- Should I take a lump sum settlement?
- Should I sue for failure to pay?
- Should I sue for future increases?

These are not easy decisions for anyone. But for the Christian who has undergone a divorce, the decisions are even more confusing. In addition to weighing traditional wisdom, a Christian must also weigh the counsel of God's Word. That wouldn't be difficult if the counsel were absolute—such as do not sue; do not hold your husband accountable for his children's expenses; etc.

Unfortunately, God's Word is not that clear and usually requires some interpretation. Furthermore, the interpretation you get often depends on who is doing the interpreting.

A counselor who relates primarily to couples who are still married will almost always say, "Wives, obey your husbands that you may win them over."

A counselor who deals with battered women or abused children will usually say, "Call the police and have him thrown in jail."

A counselor who deals with abandoned families will usually say, "Sue him for support, and throw him in jail if he doesn't pay."

Virtually every one of these Christian counselors believes in what he or she says and does. However, each is looking from a biased perspective. They are greatly influenced by the clients they see and the misery they share. I can understand that. I have often felt the same way with people I have counseled. I empathized with them, as any caring person will do.

Perhaps if I had been alive in the Lord's day and had been a disciple, I might have been tempted to raise a group of zealots and try to rescue Jesus from the Jews. But I rather suspect that had one of Jesus' followers attempted to do that, he would have been chastened, just as the Lord chastened Peter for resisting the mob that came for Him. It's important to remember: Man's way is not God's way.

Any counselor worth his time must learn to disassociate himself from his (or her) own feelings and give the counsel that is based on the best interpretation of God's Word. Many times I have listened while honest, dedicated Christians explained how other Christians they trusted had willfully cheated them and several others out of their money. Often after persistent efforts to get the issue resolved the offender simply said, "So if you don't like it, sue me."

Almost always the counselees in my office were there asking if they could do exactly that—sue the guilty spouse. They had usually already received the go-ahead from one or more other counselors, sometimes including their pastor. Emotionally I agree with the logic of suing a crook, Christian or not, who refuses all attempts to amiably settle the issue. Almost certainly these people are going to cheat someone else in the future. But the issue is not what I think, nor what any other counselor thinks. It is what God thinks! Sometimes, when the answer is not clear, several counselors are required. As Proverbs 15:22 says, "Without consultation, plans are frustrated, but with many counselors they succeed."

However, where the issue is not in doubt, only one source of counsel is required according to Proverbs 8:10, "Take my instruction, and not silver, and knowledge rather than choicest gold."

I recall an incident from several years back that helped solidify in my own mind that God's Word is the ultimate source of all decisions.

Jean was going through a bitter divorce. Her husband, Rex, had left her for a younger woman. I knew Rex from several men's Bible studies I had attended shortly after becoming a Christian. He was an able teacher and I had learned a great deal under his teaching. The only potential flaw I noticed was an overzealousness about Christianity. He set Sundays aside as a day dedicated to nothing but studying the Word for his entire family. While there is nothing wrong with that, he seemed to attack his faith as an effort in pleasing God, rather than serving Him. His messages were heavy with the need to sacrifice for the Lord, and he commented that if a Christian didn't spend at least an hour a day in prayer he was not dedicated. While I couldn't deny that what he was saying made a lot of sense, both practically and biblically, I felt he was trying to earn God's favor. I figured that if the Pharisees couldn't do that, I probably didn't have a chance. So I accepted the majority of his teaching, and just ignored the legalistic side.

When Rex left his family and filed for divorce, Jean had been advised by several other Christians to "make it tough" on Rex. He was trying to take virtually all their household items, including the furniture, their best car, a nice boat, and several other items that could be better used by Jean and their three children.

They had operated a business together for several years and he also wanted to buy out her interest, using proceeds from the business to do so (not a great deal for Jean).

Jean's question was a very honest and basic one: "Should I hold out for as much as I can get (and probably have a right to)?"

There seemed to be no doubt that the marriage was over. Rex was currently living with the younger woman and had expressed his desire to marry her as soon as possible. If anyone ever had a biblical right to divorce her husband, it was Jean. And it certainly didn't make any sense not to secure her own future since Rex had made it clear he did not intend to do so.

I really didn't know how to counsel Jean at the time. Somewhere in my mind there was a nagging feeling that Jesus probably would have told her not to hold out for all she could get. I also had a doubt that He would have advised her to countersue for divorce, as she had been advised. But my emotions told me that Rex was a self-centered hypocrite who simply dumped her for a newer model. I asked her to give me a day to pray about what counsel I could offer.

That night I spent some time in prayer, just asking the Lord to give me what He had promised—wisdom (see James

1:5). By the next morning I knew I had the answer God intended for me, and hopefully for Jean.

When we met the next day, I shared with her what I knew about the relationship between a husband and wife from God's Word. One of the first examples we have is that of Abram and Sarai in Genesis 12. Abram tried to trade Sarai to the Pharaoh because he feared for his own hide. Throughout it all she honored her husband and later was blessed by God. As you probably know, later Abraham did the same thing again.

In Ephesians 5, Paul gives the primary teaching in the New Testament on husband-wife relationships. I have heard teachers say that the instructions given in Ephesians 5 are conditional, meaning the wife should do her part only if her husband does his part. I can find no such condition in all the Bible. Marriage is a vow taken by two people to unconditionally love each other. God doesn't make *any* of the marriage instructions conditional. Each spouse is totally responsible to do what God says regardless of whether the other does or does not obey. Each of us will be accountable for our own actions when we stand before the Lord. I find this interpretation makes my decisions a lot easier when sorting them out.

We ended the session in Philippians 2:3 where Paul said, "Do nothing from selfishness or empty conceit, but with humility of mind let each of you regard one another as more important than himself," and in Philippians 3:8 where he said, "More than that, I count all things to be loss in view of the surpassing value of knowing Christ Jesus my Lord, for whom I have suffered the loss of all things, and count them but rubbish in order that I may gain Christ." I closed by asking Jean to pray about these passages and then do as she felt the Lord was leading her.

The next day she called to say that what we had discussed confirmed what she had been feeling all along. She would not countersue, and would not fight Rex for any properties. She would rely on the Lord to do the convicting for her.

I received a couple of heated calls about the "advice" I had given her. The pastor challenged my ability to give good counsel to anyone. "If that's the kind of advice you give," he said sternly, "I would suggest you keep it to yourself." The second caller, her attorney, issued a slightly veiled threat that if later she regretted the decision, I might be held liable for the advice I gave.

I explained to both of them that I had not given advice at all. I had merely helped her to reach the decision that she felt was from the Lord. If they had a problem with that, they should take it up with Him.

I would like to be able to say that every time a Christian decides to trust God and do exactly what His Word says, it works out for his or her good. I do believe that ultimately it will, but it may be in the next lifetime, not this one. The issue is not gratification in the human sense. It is obedience to our Lord. In Daniel 3, Shadrach, Meshach, and Abed-nego told Nebuchadnezzar that if he threw them into his furnace their God could rescue them from it. But then they made it clear that even if he didn't rescue them, they would not bow to his idol. They were confirming a biblical principle: God may rescue us, or He may not, but it should make no difference in our obedience.

Jean's attorney did everything he could to talk her out of her decision, as did her pastor and several close friends. They resented the idea that Rex might get away with his scheme. Jean called me a couple of times when her resolve was low, typically after she had some dealings with Rex and his attitude was particularly rotten. During one such call I told her what I believed to be the truth: "Jean, if your decision is based on expecting Rex to change, then you probably have made the wrong choice. He may never change, but that's his problem. Your decision must be based on a conviction from the Lord, not that of a counselor—me or anyone else."

One of the things I have learned by experience is that all counselors are wrong sometimes, some are wrong most of the time. The Proverbs give a good balance to remember when seeking counsel. First, Proverbs 15:22, "Without consultation, plans are frustrated, but with many counselors they succeed." This indicates that a wise person seeks the counsel of others before making critical decisions. Second, Proverbs 14:15, "The naive believes everything, but the prudent man considers his steps." This indicates that only a fool listens to most of what he hears.

At first Rex thought Jean was pulling some kind of ploy on him, so he instructed his attorney to ask for even more concessions, one of which was no alimony. Jean agreed. The only stipulation she gave was that Rex must provide child support for his children. Jean had her resolve tested many times during the next several months. When Rex came by to see the children, she treated him like a friend that had dropped by to visit. No matter what he did she tried not to react negatively.

Then one day Rex called unexpectedly and asked if he could come by. Jean agreed and later that day he arrived. She had made some coffee and asked him to come into the kitchen.

She had just poured the coffee when Rex said, "Jean, I would like to come home."

Jean almost dropped the coffee cup she was holding. Instead she took a sip and calmly asked, "Why?"

"Because I know how wrong I've been. I've been living in sin and I can't stand myself anymore. I've already been to the pastor and asked for forgiveness. I've agreed to apologize before the church and enter the new members' class."

Jean literally gulped down the scalding coffee as her heart thumped. "Are you sure this is what you want, Rex?"

"I've never been so sure of anything. I'll sleep on the couch if you want, and I wouldn't blame you if you said no. You've been so great about this and I've been a louse."

"I can't disagree," Jean said with a smile. "But I'm willing to try if you are."

It has now been nearly 10 years since the incident with Rex and Jean. They are still married and Rex has been the model of a dedicated husband. He has refused any additional leadership within the church and limits himself to counseling men who have left their families. Jean didn't really win Rex back — God did.

Each individual must ultimately decide for herself about a divorce settlement and whether or not to fight for her "rights." There are few, if any, biblical principles to guide you in these decisions simply because God hates divorce and thus doesn't prescribe rules for dissolving a marriage.

It is my personal conviction that a man is responsible for his family, including his spouse. That responsibility doesn't end simply because the law says they are no longer married. But once either party remarries, and it is no longer possible to restore the relationship, then this line of authority ends. The wife is free from his authority. The husband is still biblically responsible only for his children. The instruction given the people of Israel in Deuteronomy 24:4 is an indication of this principle.

Should You Demand the Home?
Often women in the midst of a divorce cling to their homes for security. In reality the home can be a financial weight that pulls them down. The decision to keep or sell a home should be based on a budget, not emotions. If sufficient funds are available to maintain the home for a period of time after the divorce, generally that is a matter of choice. There is always the chance that the marriage will be restored. But I have seen many divorcees literally impoverished by trying to maintain a home far beyond their budgets. The pressure to keep some residual of the marriage for the children is usually the motivation. Second to that is the idea that the home represents security for the future, or the fear that buying another home will be impossible later.

In the next chapters we will be looking at some rules of budgeting for single parents, one of which is: Make the hard decisions quickly so they don't become impossible decisions later. If the home consumes more than 30 to 35 percent of disposable income, it has to go!

Candy was in the midst of a divorce that had devastated her. She and David had been married since their second year in college and, although theirs was a stormy relationship, she had never seriously thought about a divorce. Both had good

93

jobs in the same bank. Candy was the assistant marketing director, a job high in prestige, but low in pay. They lived in a very nice home that both had contributed a lot of time and effort toward—so much so that Candy hadn't noticed the little telltale signs of David's involvement with someone else. It was only when David decided to leave that she realized he had been seeing another bank employee for nearly a year.

They had two children, a son in high school and another in junior high. As the divorce proceeded and Candy realized that David was not coming back, she clung to her home as the last sense of security. The difficulty was that to maintain the payments required two incomes. At the court hearing David agreed to pay $500 a month child support and six months alimony of $500. Unfortunately, this was enough to tempt Candy into trying to keep the home. She rationalized the decision as an effort to stabilize her children after the trauma of the divorce, and subsequent remarriage of their father.

Within a year Candy was hopelessly in debt. She had borrowed against the equity in the home to keep the payments current for the first several months. Then she attempted to remortgage in an effort to extend the inevitable a little longer. Had she decided to sell the home soon after the divorce, she could have recovered the equity of nearly $25,000. In the meantime the market had dropped because of an oil-related recession in her area and the home was worth less than the outstanding mortgages.

There was little any counselor could do except negotiate with the lender for an orderly repossession. Fortunately in her state the law prohibited surety for deficiencies on homes so she was able to get out of the home debt-free. As the Lord said in Luke 14:28, it is important to sit down, consider the entire cost, and decide if you have enough funds to complete the task. Candy's decision was made the day David was remarried; she was just unwilling to accept it then.

A Lump Sum Settlement

Hope was offered a lump sum settlement through her husband's attorney. Brian was a surgeon earning over $200,000 a year. Based on his income, his attorney figured she was entitled to child support of $1,500 a month for their three children and alimony of $1,000 a month. Since Hope had worked for five years to help put Brian through college and medical school, her attorney was also asking for an additional settlement of $2,000 a month for five years.

Their relationship was a rocky one from the beginning. Brian was a workaholic and stayed away from home most of the time. They had started out marriage on the wrong foot, with Hope pregnant. She had dropped out of nursing school just after they were married, and then she had a miscarriage and lost the baby. Almost immediately she went back to school and finished her training. Brian was a senior in premed and dedicated to being a surgeon, like his father.

Throughout medical school Hope worked and Brian spent long hours studying and interning. She complained that they never saw each other, but always assumed that would eventually change when Brian finished school.

Instead, it got progressively worse. Once out of school Brian began his residency and then received a grant to study pediatric surgery in England. By this time they had one child, with another on the way and Hope could not go with him. He commuted for nearly two years, seeing his family only once every two months at best. After his residency and certification he accepted a position with a prestigious university hospital in the Washington, D.C. area and quickly rose to become the head of pediatric surgery.

Unfortunately, each successive step put Brian more out of touch with his family. Hope began to complain and later to nag about his lack of compassion for his children (and her). To a physician who receives nothing but accolades at work and admiration from his patients, too often the stress of a family drives him further into his work. This is exactly what happened to Brian. Finally he decided to move out of the house and into an apartment.

In Hope's words, "I hardly knew the difference and the kids didn't really know their father anyway." Quickly they moved apart in what they both knew from the beginning would probably be a permanent situation. Hope had begun to drink heavily from time to time. Her mother was a daily alcoholic and it frightened her to realize she might become one too. She finally went to her best friend, Jenny, for help. Jenny recommended that she talk with their pastor, who was himself a recovering alcoholic.

During their first session together, Pastor Clemmons explained how he had become an alcoholic while running a psychological counseling business. As a trained psychologist he knew the dangers of any drug, but a nagging fear of the future led him to drink to escape the depression that haunted him.

"That's just where I am," Hope confessed. "Brian and I got married for the wrong reasons and I know he doesn't really love me. I don't seem to fit into his world and he doesn't want to fit into mine."

Pastor Clemmons asked Hope to attend a helps class that he taught one night a week for people with a dependency problem. After some initial struggles admitting she had a problem, Hope agreed to attend. The deciding factor was her alarm at the realization that she could no long fall asleep without three or four drinks every night. The thought of an even greater dependency on alcohol frightened her into swallowing her pride.

At one of the meetings several weeks later she committed her life to Christ, and was delivered from her fears and dependency on alcohol.

Hope tried to share her experience with Brian over the next few weeks, but it was clear that he neither cared nor shared her beliefs. He saw religion as just one more "crutch" needed by his weak-willed wife. His subsequent offer to settle the property side of their divorce was his way of closing that chapter in his life.

Hope knew that once their divorce was finalized Brian would buffer himself from her and the children and bury himself in his work. If he were released from any continuing responsibility, they would quite likely become victims of the old out-of-sight, out-of-mind syndrome.

She decided not to take the settlement of nearly $500,000. Instead she dropped her demands for alimony and requested an increase in child support to $2,500 a month, which would allow her to pay for an in-home sitter while she worked. Brian's attorney jumped at the offer and pressured him into agreeing as quickly as possible. Needless to say, Hope's attorney was distraught. She had traded a guaranteed income of at least $25,000 a year, plus child support, for $30,000 a year in child support for not longer than 15 years (the age of maturity for their youngest child). Hope calmly explained her reasoning on the counsel of her new pastor: "Leave the door open for God to work."

The divorce was finalized and, true to form, Brian virtually severed all ties with his family. He would send them presents on their birthdays and at Christmas, but seldom visited. Hope continued to grow in her faith and the one thing that did impress Brian was her lack of dependence on him. She took a job as a night nurse at the same hospital where he practiced and he would periodically hear reports from other nurses of her abilities and compassion. Twice she was offered a shift supervisor's position and turned it down so that she could spend more time with her children.

She also had many opportunities to date hospital staff and turned them all down, saying that she still considered herself to be married, another comment that did not go unnoticed by Brian.

Three years after their divorce, an event took place that changed Brian's life. He was involved in a very bad automobile accident that left his right arm partially paralyzed from a back injury. Abruptly his career as a surgeon ended. He continued on as chief-of-staff, but in a non-surgical role. Suddenly he found himself with surplus time on his hands, without the demands of an attending physician. For Brian, it was as if his meaning for life left him. He felt like a charity case with the hospital and his partners carrying him.

In the midst of all this he began looking for some answers. He turned to Hope for help. One evening he called and asked if he could come over to talk with her. She agreed.

"Hope, I just wanted to tell you that I have changed my will. I'm leaving everything to you and the kids," he said despondently.

"You sound like this is an epitaph," Hope said, sensing his words as those of a potential suicide.

"Maybe so," Brian replied. "I don't have anything left to live for. I messed up our marriage and now I'm no longer any good to anyone—at least not alive. Maybe my death will have some meaning; my life sure doesn't."

"I think you're about to make the biggest blunder so far," Hope said, looking him in the eyes.

"What do you mean?" Brian asked, astonished. This was a side of Hope he hadn't seen before. It was as if he were the student and she the instructor.

"Brian, haven't you wondered what it is that has given me the strength to go through these last five years?" she asked.

"Well, I know there has been a change in you," he remarked. "I guess you mean it's your religion. That's OK for you. But it's not my thing."

"Religion isn't my thing, either—as you put it," she replied defensively. "I know the Creator of this world as my Savior. That's my strength and comfort. What do you have that carries you through the trials, Brian?"

"Nothing I guess," he replied. "My whole life seems a waste now."

"That's only because you allow it to. But if you think you have problems now, just think what it will be like for eternity to realize that you made the biggest mistake of your life. You rejected the only person who can release you from your guilt and sins: the Lord Jesus Christ."

"That's OK for you, Hope. But I don't believe in God. When you die, you die—that's it."

"But what if you're wrong, Brian? Then what? Do you think you've been wrong about other things?"

"It would seem so."

"Well, stop listening to the people around you tell you how great you are because you're a doctor. We're all sinners and need help."

Hope and Brian had many more conversations like this one over the next several weeks. The evidence that Hope had peaked Brian's interest was that he didn't attempt suicide. He began to attend the helps group meetings from time to time and was impressed by the total honesty of the group, and the fact that he could be himself without any pretense. Later that year Brian committed his life to Christ and began to mature spiritually.

The change was dramatic, and he attacked his new-found faith with the same vigor that he had shown in his career as a physician. A few months later he and Hope were remarried. Brian accepted a position as head of a missions medical staff in southeast Asia, where he and Hope now live. Their children are married to Christians and each is serving in ministries throughout the world.

Certainly not all situations work out as well as Hope and Brian's. More common is that marriages fail and the parties split forever. However, I believe the key ingredient in any marriage that survives is a total surrender to the Lord.

For those divorcees facing the decision of whether or not to accept a lump sum settlement it is important to make that decision on your own, based on God's counsel in your life. It will be different for everyone. In general, I counsel a prospective divorcee not to accept a lump sum settlement, unless there is a very realistic prospect that her husband will not support his family once the divorce is finalized. The majority of women whom I have counseled who accepted lump sum settlements ended up either losing the money through bad investments or spent it during the first few years. Obviously good money management helps to avoid these situations. But just as recent widows are vulnerable to outside influences, so are recent divorcees.

Should You Sue for Nonpayment?

This is an issue that more and more women are facing in our society: Should you sue your husband for nonpayment? I would first like to discuss the simpler issue of suing for nonpayment of alimony.

Alimony is the regular monthly support assigned to one spouse (more often the husband) for the support of the other spouse, usually until the latter is remarried. In the last decade or so it is less common for a spouse to receive alimony except in cases where an enormous income is at stake, such as the divorces of entertainers, athletes, etc.

On the basis of God's Word I can see nothing that would scripturally allow a wife to sue her husband for nonpayment of alimony. I personally believe that a husband should pay to support his (ex) wife, since God does not recognize divorce. But if he will not, then the wife should not sue.

I know this counsel will run contrary to much Christian teaching, as I told you earlier that it would. I even humanly agree with the logic of suing a rascal so sorry that he won't support his wife. I have also seen, firsthand, the difficulties the lack of alimony can cause. But God's Word is not dependent on *our* human logic or approval. Just as the three Jewish disciples whose story is told in Daniel 3 had to be willing to commit themselves to the furnace, so must a Christian wife, if she is ever to tap into the power of the Lord. Sometimes the answer may not be what we would wish. Perhaps there were other young men throughout history who refused to bow and lost their lives. They are not recorded. Bear in mind the words of the Lord in Matthew 16:24-26: "Then Jesus said to His disciples, 'If anyone wishes to come after Me, let him deny himself, and take up his cross, and follow Me. For whoever wishes to save his life shall lose it; but whoever loses his life for My sake shall find it. For what will a man be profited, if he gains the whole world, and forfeits his soul? Or what will a man give in exchange for his soul?' "

The issue of child support is an entirely different matter. Unlike the parents, children have no choice in their circumstances. They didn't choose to be born to us. They were given to our care by God. A father (or mother) cannot refuse his responsibility to his children just because it is inconvenient. As Paul said in 1 Timothy 5:8, "But if anyone does not provide for his own, and especially for those of his household, he has denied the faith, and is worse than an unbeliever."

But what if the father is an unbeliever? It makes no difference at all if he says he is a believer or nonbeliever—the rules are the same. If he has fathered children, he must support them.

Bottom line, if this means using the law to force him to meet his responsibility, so be it. Prior to the mid 1970s it was possible for a parent to avoid paying child support by moving from one stateto another. Since local courts had no jurisdiction beyond state boundaries, a warrant for abandonment was not enforceable outside the state. That is no longer true. Federal legislation was passed that makes it possible to extradite a parent for abandonment, including failure to pay child support.

I recommend doing everything possible outside of filing suit for abandonment. But, all other avenues failing, a father who refuses to support his children should be arrested and jailed if necessary. If the reason for failure to pay is beyond his control (illness, unemployment, etc.), that obviously should be taken into account. But remember, everybody can pay something, even if it is not everything.

Future Increases

It is common for a divorcee to take her husband back to court periodically to secure more income for herself or the children. The issue of "to sue or not to sue" should be clear, from a biblical perspective. If it involves alimony, a wife should not sue. If it involves child support, the decision must be made on the basis of actual need, not anger or greed. Be certain that all other means of negotiating have been exhausted before appealing to the courts for assistance. And be certain that your motive is need—not revenge or greed. "Let your character [way of life] be free from love of money, being content with what you have; for He Himself has said, 'I will never desert you, nor will I ever forsake you' " (Hebrews 13:5).

■ 7 A PRACTICAL BUDGET

Just the mention of the word *budget* arouses negative feelings in some people. They see a budget as means of restricting their fun and freedom. In reality the exact opposite is true. A budget is merely a plan whereby you decide how you are going to spend the money you have. It also helps to determine when you have spent all you can without the risk of going into debt.

One of the most common statements I hear from single parents is, "I don't really make enough to budget." What that actually means is that when they balance how much they need to live on against how much they have coming in, the numbers don't come close.

My comment usually is, "Suppose I have someone who wants to make up your deficit. How will you be able to tell them how much you actually need?"

That usually gets them to thinking. Often the response is, "Well, I think I need about ($200) a month to make it."

My next question is, "If you had the funds and were willing to help, would you give to someone who guesses about what he needs, or would you give to the person who can demonstrate the need on paper?"

The response is about what you would anticipate. Obviously if we are going to help someone, we would expect that person to show an actual need. And we would want to be certain that he or she was handling the available funds as well as possible. That is all a budget can or should do.

God has promised to meet our needs. But as best I know, He no longer drops manna from heaven. In most instances He uses people to whom He has given a surplus to help the less fortunate. As James 2:15-16 says, "If a brother or sister is without clothing and in need of daily food, and one of you says to them, 'Go in peace, be warmed and be filled'; and yet you do not give them what is necessary for their body; what use is that?"

The people who willingly surrender a part of their assets to help others would themselves be poor stewards if they required no accountability from those they help. I personally would not give money to anyone (other than an emergency) who was not involved in some type of financial counseling and living on a budget. After all, I live on a budget too.

A budget, to be of any value, must be as uncomplicated as possible and still get the job done. When I first began to counsel, I checked out every budget workbook in the stores. I knew I needed something to help the counselees get started, and it had to be simple. If most of them had been able to keep detailed financial records, they probably wouldn't have needed me in the first place. What I discovered was that the budget books available at that time were designed *by* accountants *for* accountants—or at least that's the way it seemed. They were thick books with lots of complicated forms and practically no pictures or examples.

So as I started out to design my own budget workbook, I asked myself, what is the simplest budgeting system available? The answer was deceptively simple—using envelopes to keep your money in.

For instance, if you converted your total income each pay period to cash, divided it into the categories of your spending, and put it in envelopes, you would have a rudimentary budget. As the payments or expenditures came due, you would only need to draw the money out of the applicable envelope (housing, auto, clothing, insurance, etc.) and pay the bills. Of course you could always rob one envelope to pay for something you wanted in another category. But then, no budget will control overspending. Only you can do that!

The key to the envelope budget is that when an envelope is empty you stop spending in that category until the next paycheck.

One more step is necessary if your envelope budget system is to last beyond the next few months: You must anticipate expenses that don't come due every month, such as annual insurance, taxes, car repairs, vacations, gifts, Christmas spending, etc. Then you must allocate these nonmonthly expenditures in other envelopes that will be kept until the expense arises. It is most often these little unplanned expenses that will destroy a budget and convince the budgeter that it won't work.

Although I have helped many people develop an envelope budgeting system when I found they could not manage a checking account, I don't recommend it for most people. It's not a good idea to leave that much cash in your home. And learning to maintain a checkbook is not difficult at all — with a little help and a few simple rules.

The budgeting system I have used for many years now is based on the envelope system except that all of the noncurrent spending funds are kept in a checking account. We substitute individual account sheets for the envelopes and a running balance is kept on each category of spending, i.e., housing, auto, food, etc. In other words, all spending decisions are done based on what is in your account sheets — not your checking account. The total balance of all the account sheets will equal what is in the checking account.

INDIVIDUAL ACCOUNT FORM

	$	$
ACCOUNT CATEGORY	ALLOCATION	ALLOCATION

DATE	TRANSACTION	DEPOSIT	WITHDRAWAL	BALANCE

For example, if you need clothes for your child, you don't look to see if there is any money left in the checking account. Instead you look at the clothing allocation sheet to see if there is any money left in it. Otherwise you will be spending funds that were allocated to another area.

For those categories that cannot be funded because of a lack of money, you have a very specific prayer request. And if the Lord prompts someone to ask about your needs, you will have specific facts to give them. I have often seen the Lord bless a good steward who was managing well what he or she had but simply lacked the funds needed for nonmonthly expenses.

In the rest of the chapter I would like to cover a basic budget, category by category, and offer some suggestions on how to budget on a single parent's income. The assumption I have made is that you fit the average single parent's profile: a mother, divorced with two children, living on $13,000 to $15,000 a year gross income.

The first important principle to know in budgeting is how much "spendable income" you have available. Often the percentages that are given for categories like housing and auto are based on gross (total) income. This never made any sense to me, since no one actually has their gross income to spend: only net income. So the percentages I will use are after taxes and tithes (assuming that you tithe). This will be called your "Net Spendable Income."

GROSS INCOME PER MONTH   _____
    Salary   _____
    Interest   _____
    Dividends   _____
    Other   _____

LESS:
1. Tithe   _____

2. Tax (Est. – Incl. Fed., State, FICA)   _____

NET SPENDABLE INCOME   _____

Know What You Spend

Once you know how much you have available to budget, the next step is to find out how much you are presently spending. You can do this in either of two ways. One, go through your checkbook for the previous year and divide out your spending by the categories we will discuss. This presumes you do the majority of your spending out of your checking account, and you don't write one check for multiple categories (such as writing a check for groceries and cash together). Otherwise this method won't work for you. You'll have to go to plan "B."

The second method is to keep a diary for a least one month listing everything you buy, category by category. There will be some expenses that are not incurred every month, such as car repairs, clothes, vacations, etc. These must be estimated based on some average spending estimates.

Let's assume at this point you know how much you have available to spend, and you know (within reason) how much you spend monthly, but the two don't match. The next step is to look at each category of spending to decide if some adjustments can be made. By looking at each spending category, you can brainstorm ideas to help you budget better. If, after doing all you can to control your spending, you still cannot make your budget balance, you qualify as needy and require the support of other Christians. If your church does not have an active single parents' benevolence plan, then you need to pray and help get one started.

The Budget Categories

• *Category 1—Taxes.* Everybody has to pay taxes, divorcees with inadequate income included. The amount of taxes paid will vary based on income and expenses, but the one tax virtually no one can escape is Social Security (FICA). If you work for someone else, these taxes are taken out before you are paid. But if you are self-employed through child care services in your home, outside sales of direct marketing products (such as Amway, Mary Kay cosmetics, and so on), you are required to pay Social Security self-employment taxes on income up to approximately $50,000 per year.

Unlike the FICA taken from an employee's pay, which is one-half the total paid in, the entire amount is assessed to the self-employed. There are tax breaks available as of 1990, but that is not a subject of this book. You should contact a good local accountant about any tax questions you might have.

I addressed the subject of taxes here only because in counseling I have often encountered divorcees who owed substantial amounts to the IRS because they failed to pay on self-employed income. The direct marketing plans used in home businesses are usually the primary source of self-employment income.

I estimate that the average divorcee making $15,000 a year will owe approximately 10 percent of her gross income in all taxes.

So remember, you started out with $1,250 a month (based on a $15,000 per year income). You are now down to $1,125.

GROSS INCOME	= $15,000/Year	$1,250/Month
LESS TAXES	− 1,500/Year	125/Month
	$13,500/Year	$1,125/Month

• *Category 2 — Tithes.* I have often been asked whether a Christian (who happens to be a divorced mother) should tithe if her income is already inadequate to meet all her family's needs. Let me summarize what I believe God's Word teaches on this subject, then let God do the convicting.

The tithe is meant to be an outside, material indicator that God owns everything in our lives. The first tithe recorded in Scripture was by Abraham in Genesis 14:20, who gave Melchizedek the priest a tenth of all the spoils of battle as a symbol of his gratitude to God for victory. In Hebrews 7:1-9 we are told that Abraham gave this tithe (430 years before the Law came) in order to acknowledge God's ownership over all that he had.

In Proverbs 3:9-10 we are told to "honor" God from the best of our resources. "Honor the Lord from your wealth, and from the first of all your produce; so your barns will be filled with plenty, and your vats will overflow with new wine." I truly believe that God doesn't need the money, nor is He an accountant checking to see if we're careful to give exactly a tenth. God checks the heart attitude and blesses accordingly. If you don't feel the desire to give, then don't. As the Apostle Paul said in 2 Corinthians 9:7, "Let each one do just as he has purposed in his heart; not grudgingly or under compulsion; for God loves a cheerful giver."

For those who elect to tithe, I will assume that 10 percent goes to the Lord's work. This leaves you with 80 percent of the original income or $1,000 per month: So that's *all* that can be spent—total.

NET INCOME (After Taxes)	=	$13,500/Year	$1,125/Month
LESS TITHE	−	1,500/Year	125/Month
NET SPENDABLE INCOME	=	$12,000/Year	$1,000/Month

Spending Categories

The percentages we will discuss for the next categories all relate to your net spendable income (after taxes and tithe). Therefore, their total will equal 100 percent.

• *Category 3—Housing.* The maximum percentage that can be allocated to housing is approximately 35 percent of NSI (Net Spendable Income), or $350 per month. This includes your payments or rent, utilities (including telephone), taxes, maintenance, literally everything associated with housing—including insurance.

Since we have already discussed this topic earlier, I won't spend more time here. The critical factor is: Don't overspend on housing.

• *Category 4—Food.* This is food that you buy at a grocery store or its equivalent. It does not include eating out or entertaining. Eating out is allocated under entertainment expenses. The maximum percent of NSI that can be allocated to food is approximately 15 percent, or $150 per month. As you must already realize, this is not much money for food for a family of two or three. However, if you elect to spend more in this category, it will have to come out of some other area of your budget.

For most single parents, making the food budget work means shopping discount stores, clipping coupons, hunting specials, buying dented cans, and a myriad of other ideas to reduce costs.

It probably also means that you will need to eliminate most

"junk foods," including potato chips, cookies, soft drinks, and the like. It will also mean no prepared foods, such as micro-wave-ready meals and frozen dinners. The cost of labor in these items is too expensive for most budgets. But take heart, when I grew up these things weren't even thought about yet. Your kids will survive without them, and probably live longer, healthier lives too.

• *Category 5—Automobile Expenses.* Your budget can handle approximately 15 percent for all auto-related expenses. This gives you $150 per month for everything, including pay-ments, insurance, maintenance, gas, and replacement.

As I noted earlier, this is one of those categories where you will need to be extremely disciplined and trust God for what you cannot provide yourself. Basically, without some intervention from outside your own budget, it will not work. Most single parents do not have the income to replace their worn-out cars. And they certainly don't have the income to buy new ones. This is one of the major sources of debt for single parents. Make an absolute commitment that you will not buy a car you can't afford, and you will not use credit cards to buffer your car repair expenses. I have known many people who did and it never gets easier later. Appendix F contains some helpful information on selecting and evaluating the right car for you.

• *Category 6—Insurance.* This includes all insurance not as-sociated with housing or automobile. Your budget can handle approximately 5 percent for this category, just $50 per month. In order to make this category stretch you must prioritize your insurance needs, the greatest of which is health insurance while your children are at home. Unless you have access to a group insurance plan at work, the cost of health insurance is beyond the reach of most single parents.

HEALTH INSURANCE

Alternatives are available if you don't have a company-paid group plan. One is a group called the "Brotherhood Associa-tion." This is an association of Christians who have banded together to provide a self-insured health plan for those who cannot normally get other coverage. The average monthly cost per family is about $75 (as of late 1990). Unfortunately that is above this category's allocation but it may be prudent to sacrifice in another area of your budget to control your health care costs. If you would like to contact the Brotherhood Association, write them at: 6680 Taylor Road, Clinton, Ohio 44216-9033.

Another similar group is the Good Samaritan Program (P.O. Box 279, Beech Grove, Indiana 46107). However, this group functions more like a traditional insurance plan available through associations. The average monthly costs are about the same.

In a real pinch you may want to investigate Medicaid benefits. Many states have adopted rules for Medicaid that make it available to lower income families and any children under age six. I personally object to any Christians being forced to take government aid. Although I don't see any specific scriptural prohibition against accepting government aid, I do believe it reflects poorly upon the integrity of the other Christians who have a surplus they could share. As the Apostle Paul said in 2 Corinthians 8:14, "At this present time your abundance being a supply for their want, that their abundance also may become a supply for your want, that there may be equality."

LIFE INSURANCE

Many single parents worry about having no life insurance in the event of their deaths. This is a valid concern but life insurance should be a lower priority than health coverage, with limited dollars. If you can free even a small amount per month for life insurance, I suggest buying the least expensive type available. This is normally annual renewable term insurance, which means the premiums increase annually. It accumulates no cash values and is normally called "pure insurance." It provides the greatest death benefit for the least current cost. Concern yourself with investments and retirement benefits later. At this point *provision* must be your primary concern.

One additional thought on the subject of life insurance is

necessary. Many single parents worry about not having any insurance on their children in the event of a child's death. I recommend that you investigate the "Memorial Society" as a possible alternative. This is a nonprofit group out of suburban Washington, D.C. that helps to establish other nonprofit groups who in turn contract with various funeral homes throughout the nation to provide inexpensive burials. The fee to join is approximately $50 per family and burial costs average about $500. The costs will vary by state and by area. If you are interested in this program you can write: Continental Association of Funeral and Memorial Societies, Inc., 7910 Woodmont Avenue, Suite 1208, Bethesda, Maryland 20814. Other types of insurance such as disability are generally too expensive for a single parent to even consider. If you have additional funds to spend, you might investigate this area, but remember that the vast majority of people are not going to become disabled. In the event of total disability, Social Security will provide benefits if you have been in the program at least 20 quarters (five years). Additional information on Social Security benefits is provided in Appendix C.

• *Category 7—Debts.* In addition to payments on a home or car, the average single parent can handle no more than 5 percent of net spendable income on all debt payments (about $50 per month). "That's fine," you say. "But what happens if I owe $150 a month to creditors?"

In reality you cannot pay that much of your income to creditors and still make your budget balance on a $15,000 per year income (or less). If you have promised more than a maximum of 10 percent of your net income to creditors, there are three potential solutions (I assume here that a maximum of 10 percent could be worked into the average single's budget):

(1) After making out a budget that allows for the normal monthly living expenses, contact each creditor with a plan for how much you can pay them. Never promise more than you can realistically pay. You can always pay more when it is possible, but it's very hard to cut back on what has already been promised.

(2) Use an intermediary counselor such as one of the Christian Financial Concepts volunteer counselors or the Consumer Credit Counseling Service counselors program. Information on these services are available by calling Christian Financial Concepts at (404) 534-1000, or the National Foundation for Consumer Credit at (301) 589-5600.

(3) File for bankruptcy protection under Chapter Thirteen of the Federal Bankruptcy Act. This provides court protection while you are attempting to pay back the debts you have incurred. Information on the Federal Bankruptcy Act is available in my book *Debt-Free Living* (Moody Press, 1989).

Any action taken to offset the pressures of creditors must always be weighed against the principles given in God's Word. The first is that God wants His people to honor their commitments: "It is better that you should not vow than that you should vow and not pay" (Ecclesiastes 5:5). The second is that God's people must always repay a legitimate debt: "The wicked borrows and does not pay back, but the righteous is gracious and gives" (Psalm 37:21).

I have seen many situations where payment of existing obligations seemed impossible. But once the individuals made the absolute commitment to repay what was legitimately due, God provided the means to do so. I particularly like the promise found in Psalm 50:14-15: "Offer to God a sacrifice of thanksgiving, and pay your vows to the Most High; and call upon Me in the day of trouble; I shall rescue you, and you will honor Me." So you do your part and God will do His part. It won't always be an instantaneous solution, but the old adage is still true: *God is rarely early, but never late.*

• *Category 8—Entertainment and Recreation.* Usually when a budget is tight and bills are past-due, the first thing to go is all entertainment. Unfortunately, since no one can really live without some occasional recreation, even if it is just eating a hamburger out now and then, the effect is to spend outside the budget. This usually means the misuse of credit cards, and more debt.

A normal budget with all the other categories in balance can allocate about 5 percent of net spendable income for entertainment and recreation. But even a tight budget must allocate something each month. I would recommend allocating at least $10 per week – no matter what. The last thing you want is for your children to look at life as one great sacrifice of all enjoyment. Often they will associate the sacrifice with your faith and assume that to be a Christian means the total abandonment of fun. The best way to combat such a consequence is to be totally honest about your finances and to set aside at least a small amount for this category.

If you're open to God's leading, He can supply your needs even in the area of entertainment and recreation. For several years I counseled a divorcee with three children who never had any available funds for entertainment, yet God always seemed to provide. One year she was asked by her church to head up a youth group summer mission to a sister church in England. Another year she was invited to travel with the seniors group to Europe. Still another she was selected to lead a Bible study during a summer missions building trip to Canada. She was able to take her children on all these trips and share with them the joy of God's miraculous provision. This doesn't mean that God works the same way with everyone. But I do believe that most people also never allow God the right to decide such issues.

• *Category 9 – Clothing.* On a budget of $15,000 a year (gross income) you should allocate about 5 percent of your net income for clothing (about $50 per month). Two things are apparent at first glance. First, most single parents don't have $50 a month in their budget for clothing. Second, even if they did, $50 won't go very far today for two or three people.

The principle here is to at least allocate something on a monthly basis for replacement of clothes, and to eliminate all use of credit cards to buy clothes you cannot afford. Allow God to provide some of your needs from the surpluses of other people. There are many (too many) Christians who have large clothing budgets, and consequently have clothes in their closets that they virtually never wear. If you have a helps program within your church, many people will make clothes available to those who have a need. Unfortunately pride often gets in the way of the needy and they won't let their needs be known.

I remember well the comments of several divorced parents I have counseled. They said that members of their churches took the position that if they helped someone, they expected them to look needy (or seedy). In reality, most of the single parents bought their clothes only on sale. Many had one or two women in the church who provided them with clothes, especially for their children. Too often the people who reviewed the benevolence fund activities saw them as overdressed.

Let me say here that such an attitude is highly judgmental, petty, and contrary to the Word of God. In Philippians 2:3 Paul says, "Do nothing from selfishness or empty conceit, but with humility of mind let each of you regard one another as more important than himself." The people who judge others in need only by outside appearance are selfish and self-serving. I have seen many well-dressed single parents who either made their own clothes or shopped outlets and surplus stores diligently. These people should be applauded, not criticized. If you're not buying at your creditors' expense, don't hesitate to dress as well as you can. Also don't hesitate to share what you've learned with others around you. Some of the best dressed, most affluent people in our churches could use a good dose of conviction themselves.

• *Category 10—Savings.* There are always additional costs in a budget that cannot be anticipated. Therefore some additional savings are needed. I realize that in a budget where the regular monthly expenses are not being met, a savings account seems like wishful thinking. But until some savings are accumulated for the "emergencies," the use of credit cards is a certainty. It is better money management to repair refrigerators and washing machines with your own money rather than a creditor's.

The allocation for this category should be about 5 percent of spendable income. If, however, you can't put that much aside, then save whatever you can but make a commitment to start saving something!

One way to do this is to allocate a percentage of all additional income to your budgeted savings. This means cash gifts, overtime income, bonuses, garage sale profits, etc. Once you make a commitment to becoming totally debt-free, God can bless you in many ways. But if you never make the commitment, the additional money will likely always be spent. There always seem to be inexhaustible needs in the lives of single parents. Even so, savings must become an absolute priority.

• *Category 11—Medical and Dental Expenses.* The allocation for doctor bills should be at least 5 percent. Unfortunately this is one of those categories that causes havoc in most single parents' budgets. Even if you are covered by a hospitalization plan through your job, often the deductible is beyond your budget. To most single parents it seems that their children are always ill. And to some extent this is true because they are usually in daycare centers and exposed to all the illnesses of the other children.

As we discussed earlier, there are no simple solutions to this problem without the help of other people. When your out-of-pocket medical and dental expenses exceed your ability to pay, you must let the other Christians around you know it! There should be no more hesitation to share such financial needs than there would be to share a physical need.

In working with many single parents I have found that most Christian physicians and dentists will gladly provide low or even no-cost care if they are aware of your circumstances and know you are working with a trained counselor. I would encourage you to be totally honest with them upfront. Don't run up large medical bills and then tell them; let the decision to help be theirs.

Sometimes it is possible to work out a barter for much of the health care your family needs. I have known women who cleaned offices, provided tutoring, baby-sitting, and many other exchanges of labor for the medical and dental care their family needed. You really won't know unless you ask.

• *Category 12—Miscellaneous.* This is the category that contains everything that won't fit into any other category. It includes allowances, cash you carry, lunches, cosmetics, haircuts, etc. The allocation for such expenses is about 5 percent. Unless you diligently control your spending for miscellaneous items, they can consume a great deal of money. The only way I have ever found to control miscellaneous spending is to allocate only a given amount of money and then stick to it. If you run out before the next pay period, you must learn to do without.

One of the largest expenses within this category is that of gifts, including birthdays, Christmas, and any other celebration. Many single parents (and couples) go deeply into debt for gifts, often because of guilt they feel over the sacrifices of their children. Don't fall into this trap! The short-term gratification of gift giving won't balance the long-term stress of debt.

Single parents who make a commitment to manage their money correctly must develop some alternatives, such as crafts, to provide the gifts they need. Children won't feel deprived because of less gift giving. It's only because of our indulgence-crazy society that children (and parents) have the unrealistic expectations they do today. We can all stand to do some soul searching about the indulgent gifts we think children "need."

For several years when our children were small we made crafts for gifts. I can honestly say that I don't have one single gift my children ever bought me but I still have several of those they made me. We live in a generation with a warped sense of values. Teach your children that it takes more love to make gifts than it does to buy them.

• *Category 13 — Child Care.* The normal allocation for this category is 10 percent of net income. If you have been adding up the various categories, you will note that there are no percentages remaining for child care. This is because it is not a normal expenditure for most singles, even single parents. About 40 percent of single parents have to face the financial burden of daily child care. The others either have parents who help, work in the home, or don't work at a steady job.

There is no magical formula to making child care expenses

fit into your budget. It's a matter of taking the necessary funds out of the other categories. When looking at 100 percent of spending it looks simple enough to subtract 10 percent for child care expenses, until you get down to which category to reduce. Then you may well decide that it's impossible. But it has to be done if your budget is ever to balance.

The logical categories to reduce are as follows:

Housing: As difficult as it is, this category can be reduced by 5 percent or so. In some areas of the country it's relatively simple. In others there is no way to reduce single family housing costs to $300 a month. Virtually the only option is to look for another single mother to share housing costs.

Food, clothing, savings, entertainment, insurance and *auto* can all be reduced by 1 percent to free the additional funds needed. It won't be simple, but it is possible.

Steps in Budgeting

You will find an outline for beginning a budget in Appendix A of this book. This information is taken from *The Financial Planning Workbook* published by Moody Press. If you need more detailed information or copies of the actual forms used, you should be able to find this workbook in your local Christian bookstore.

Long-Range Planning

Two often-asked questions by single parents are, "How will I ever be able to send my child to college?" And, "What will I be able to do about retirement?"

There are no simple answers to these questions except what the Lord said in Matthew 6:34, "Therefore do not be anxious for tomorrow; for tomorrow will care for itself. Each day has enough trouble of its own." If you commit yourself to becoming the best steward that you can be right now, that's the best you can do. If God wants your children to have a college education, He can and will provide. The same is true of retirement. You don't want to be slothful and ignore the future, but you are only responsible to do what you can do — not what you cannot.

As your children are old enough to begin earning their own money, start them on a budget of their own with a portion of all they earn set aside for long-term goals such as education. They can earn a substantial portion of what they will need later if you will help them get started early enough. After all, that used to be the normal way to go to college only a generation ago.

A small amount saved regularly can amount to a great deal of money. For instance, assume your child started saving $10 a month at age 10, increased that to $20 a month at age 13, then to $30 a month from age 15 until college age (18). Assuming it was invested in U.S. Series "E" bonds and used for college so the earnings would be tax free, they would have nearly $3,000 available. It's not all they will need, but it's a good start.

In the next section of the book we're going to deal with the financial needs of widows. I would encourage all single parents to read this material as well. Most of it is applicable to all singles who are raising a family because it covers subjects such as wills and trusts, insurance, investment planning, and many other areas.

SECTION TWO

WIDOWS

■ 8 A WARNING FOR WIDOWS

As of 1990 the average age at which a woman is widowed is 52 years old. Statistically, approximately 82 percent of all married women will be widowed at least once in their lifetimes. Having mentioned these statistics at a conference not long ago one of the male attendees spoke up asking, "Does that mean if I divorce my wife at 51 that I will live longer?" No, it doesn't work that way! But what it does mean is that a wise man (wise with the wisdom of God) will train his wife to be his successor since he knows the likelihood is good that he will predecease her.

Most people, Christians included, don't like to discuss death, and so they delay talking about it until it's too late. If more women in the church who are widowed would speak up about some of their problems, other women would probably feel more motivated to deal with the possibility of being widowed.

The husbands who die don't always die of natural causes like heart attacks (the most common cause) or cancer (the second most common) or even diseases such as diabetes, pneumonia, etc. In our mobile society it is common for a man to die by accident. In my counseling with widows I found nearly half of all those I counseled had lost husbands by accident. My personal statistics are somewhat slanted because the younger widows (of working husbands) are more prone to seek help than are those who are widowed at an older age. Before getting into a discussion of what a widow needs to know when her husband dies, I would like to present some examples from my counseling. The names are changed, for obvious reasons, but the people are real; so are the problems.

Nate and Sherri Long had come in for budget counseling after attending a seminar at their church. Nate worked for a major company and made a good salary, but creeping inflation had raised their standard of living to where they were going into debt a little more each year. They were determined to get their finances under control and worked hard at analyzing where they were overspending and how to control it. Their problem turned out to be primarily related to vacation over-runs and two fairly new automobiles, each with sizable payments. They put the newest car up for sale, intending to use the proceeds to retire all their credit card debt and eliminate one car note. They never made it.

Nate was returning from a business trip and caught a Southern Airways flight out of Memphis to Atlanta. On the leg from Memphis to Atlanta the plane ran into some bad weather and due to an apparent error on the part of a flight controller the pilot was routed directly into the path of a severe thunderstorm. As the plane entered the storm cell it encountered heavy hail and violent turbulence. The hail clogged the twin engines of the DC-9 and both engines seized up. Sixty-three passengers lost their lives on that flight. One of them was Nate Long.

Suddenly Sherri found herself a widow at age 32. Nate had taken the time to prepare a will as a result of our counseling. He had also written Sherri a letter detailing all their assets, the total value of his insurance and government pension, and had named their attorney as co-trustee for the testimentary trust that had been drafted only weeks before Nate's death.

At about the same time Nate and Sherri came for help, another couple, Allen and Nancy Feller, also came in for counseling. Allen was a successful architect on contract with the federal government. Their income was in the $100,000 range annually but because of a series of bad investments, they owed nearly $75,000 in unsecured bank loans. They also lived in a home that consumed more than half of Allen's salary and drove two leased, and very expensive, imported cars. The net result was that Nancy had to go to work just to provide enough income for basic necessities.

Allen's attitude was, "I can work out from under this. I'm young, in good health, and my income will increase." Nancy saw the trend toward greater spending with every salary in-crease—with no apparent end to it. She practically demanded that they go for counseling after Allen lost another $10,000 on an opal mine deal in Brazil. Allen attended the counseling session out of deference to Nancy, but left all the work to her.

Allen was flying first class in the plane from Memphis when it encountered the thunderstorm. He also died that day. Over the next two years I had a chance to work with other advisers helping both Sherri and Nancy. Their stories are examples of what good and poor planning can do.

Once the shock of Nate's death wore off and the funeral was completed, Sherri called to ask for an appointment. In one notebook Nate had assembled all their insurance policies, their agent's name and address, the name of their family attorney, and all information necessary to file for Social Security survivor's benefits, as well as his veteran's benefits. In one two-hour session we had completed all the required forms and had them ready to mail.

The next week we met with Nate's insurance agent and filed for his insurance proceeds. We also filed for temporary benefits from workman's compensation since Nate had been killed while on business for his employer. The insurance company forwarded $10,000 for living and funeral expenses immediately and Sherri was able to establish a somewhat normal household routine. Also pending was a settlement from the airlines and the Federal Aviation Administration as a result of the plane crash. As it turned out, the settlement got tied up in court for the next four years. With her budget well established and enough money coming in from Social Security and workman's compensation to live on, Sherri had no abnormal financial pressures.

On the other hand, Nancy's situation went from bad to worse. Allen left no will and although Nancy was assured a portion of the estate by state law, she could receive as little as a child's share. With the large settlement from the airlines and FAA pending, the judge was not willing to assign her more than the legal limit. Potential heirs filed petitions with the court and Nancy was forced to hire attorneys to protect her interests. Since Allen worked for the government he had no Social Security benefits available. The government did continue his salary without interruption, but after six months they threatened to sue Nancy for recovery of the funds, saying that her compensation should have been paid by workman's compensation. The sum that workman's compensation would have paid was substantially less than his salary, so Nancy was facing another lawsuit, in addition to that brought on by Allen's creditors.

Over the next two years I witnessed firsthand the difficulties experienced by widows. Both suffered from emotional shock, as almost everyone does in their circumstances. However, Nancy's situation was magnified by the stress of her financial pressures. By the time the court case was settled both widows received a settlement of nearly one million dollars. Sherri was able to give a substantial portion of hers to the church, set up a college trust fund for her children, and invested the rest to provide a comfortable income.

Nancy paid 40 percent of her settlement in attorney fees. Creditors took another $200,000, and the government settled for $40,000 in back pay. Obviously she still had enough to live on but almost immediately she invested a substantial portion with a friend from her church and lost nearly $200,000 over the next two years. In the end she was forced into the job market to support herself and her two children. I attribute much of her troubles to Allen's lack of planning, and her lack of adequate training.

The Most Important Decision a Widow Can Make!

Before discussing the most important decision, let me first back up and make a comment directed to those reading this book who are not yet widowed. You may not believe any of this will ever happen to you, but believe it! Your circumstances can change literally overnight. The best decision you and your husband will ever make is to ensure you know how to manage money properly.

There are many women who never have learned to balance a checkbook, keep a budget, or make an investment decision. Clearly that is bad stewardship on the part of both the husband and wife. Every woman should keep the family's budget for at least one year, including balancing the checkbook and all the other little details that make up the finances of a family. In addition, you need to learn enough to make some critical financial decisions, such as:

• Would it be better to receive a lump sum settlement or an annuity in the event of your husband's death?

• Will you need an attorney to settle his estate or can you do it yourself?

• Where should you invest your long-term surpluses and how much ought you risk in any one place?

If you don't know how to do these things, just keep on reading because we're going to cover each of them.

Now, the single most important decision that any recent widow can make is to make *no* decisions—whether about investments, loans, new cars, or anything else that might jeopardize her assets—for at least one year. That basically means parking any money you have in an insured savings account and living off the interest, if possible. There are a myriad of other lesser decisions that we will discuss that can save you from losses, but investing or lending money in the first year can cost you everything. That is the time when a widow is the most vulnerable and therefore the most susceptible to bad advice or outright fraud. That first year should be spent getting adjusted to your new life and educated on the ins and outs of money management.

Pressured by Friends

Catherine was widowed at age 58. Her husband, Leon, had owned and operated a profitable business with a Christian partner for several years before his death. She had practically no preparation for his death. He came home one evening complaining of acute indigestion, ate dinner, then complained he was feeling worse. After a call to their family doctor he was told to go to the local hospital emergency room for tests. Two hours later he died of a massive coronary.

Once the details of the funeral were taken care of, Leon's partner explained about their buy-sell agreement that was totally funded by a life insurance plan. Within a month Catherine received nearly $700,000—in cash. Almost immediately "helpful" people began coming out of the woodwork.

First it was her son who needed to borrow $100,000 to buy into a business. Catherine loaned him the money with a promise that he would begin repaying it at 6 percent interest in six months. Shortly after that he showed up with a new convertible. When Catherine asked about it, he said it was necessary because of his new position and the "image" it required.

Then a financial planner from her church told her about an "absolutely secure" investment that would earn her 30 to 40 percent interest per year. It was supposedly a plan to lend money to major corporations for a short time. In exchange they would pay the maximum interest on the money. Catherine invested $250,000 with him after talking to her pastor, who also had invested ($1,000) in this deal.

Then came the building program at her church—timed around her recent inheritance. They needed $250,000 for a youth center, for which the church would issue bonds to Catherine paying 12 percent. She made the loan, in addition to gifting another $25,000 from her initial $700,000. She was now down to just $75,000, barely enough to use as operating capital until these investments began to pay off.

The first crack in Catherine's financial dike came when her son told her he would not be able to start paying the money back as promised. It seemed the business was having some financial problems just then. In fact, it seemed he had bought into a desperately leveraged company that had virtually no chance to pull out of its downward spiral. The owner had used Catherine's money to pay off his personal debts, knowing the business would eventually fail and he would need a fresh start.

The second shock came when the planner from her church told her he needed another $100,000 to cover the "options" he had bought in her name, or her entire investment would be lost. Unwittingly, Catherine had signed a power-of-attorney with this man who then used her money to trade commodities, in hopes of making a fortune. When Catherine couldn't come up with the money, the exchange liquidated his positions and she was presented with a bill for nearly $100,000 to cover his losses.

Catherine was still reeling from the losses she had sustained when the pastor called. We'll pick up their conversation there.

"Catherine, this is Pastor Collins. I need to discuss something with you. Is this a good time?"

"I guess so," Catherine replied with a sinking feeling inside. She had heard from the pastor twice since her husband died — once when he suggested the church bonds for the youth center, and today. She knew something must be wrong.

"I'm afraid we're not meeting the budget right now and we won't be able to pay you the interest this month. But I anticipate that giving will pick up after the youth center is completed. Don't you worry though, the church will make good on its obligations. You wouldn't want us to divert money from missions just to pay your interest, would you?"

"No, I guess not," Catherine replied without a lot of conviction.

"Good, I just knew you would understand. It's not like you can't afford the delay, I know. The Lord has provided bountifully for you."

"Yes," Catherine agreed weakly.

When the pastor hung up, Catherine just sat there crying. In less than a year she had lost virtually all that her husband left her. Nearly 20 years of Leon's hard work gone, she thought despondently.

A Grace-ful No

Grace was married to Richard for nearly 30 years when he was killed in an automobile accident coming home from his office one day. Richard owned and operated a successful sales representative company and was known throughout the business as a good organizer and trainer. His accomplishments didn't end when office hours were over either. He had helped Grace learn all about good budget management in the home and consulted with her about virtually every major business decision. As they had more funds to invest he had sent Grace to college to study real estate, business management, and the fundamentals of good investing.

Richard had executed a buy-sell agreement with his team of salespeople and upon his death they opted to buy the company for $600,000 in cash. When they ran into difficulty arranging financing for the total amount, Grace made a counter offer: an $800,000 purchase price with $400,000 cash and she would finance the remainder for five years. She met with the group and convinced them that it was a better deal since they could actually pay the note off from company profits—assuming they operated the business as successfully as Richard had. They agreed and signed the note.

With the $400,000 from the sale of the business and another $250,000 from Richard's life insurance, Grace knew that she could be financially comfortable for the rest of her life. If the $400,000 note paid off, that was great. But even if it fell through for some reason, she would have no financial problems.

But that wasn't enough for Grace. She and Richard had supported many ministries from their income over the years and she wanted to continue that practice. Upon my advice she agreed to park her money for one year, after giving the Lord's share, as she termed it. During that time she would investigate all the options available to her and decide how much risk she could prudently assume.

During that first year she was contacted by people selling everything from soap to high-interest zero coupon bonds. But since she had tied up her funds in time deposits she had a simple rebuff: "Sorry, but my money is completely tied up." Her daughter and son-in-law approached her about investing some money (about $200,000) into his business. Since her funds were totally illiquid, she could honestly say: "Sorry, my funds are totally tied up." He borrowed the money from a friend's retirement account and before the year was out had lost the company and the funds.

After the year waiting period Grace had identified several things she wanted to invest in. She decided to limit all speculative investing to no more than $200,000 in increments of no more than $15,000 each, in compliance with Solomon's instruction in Ecclesiastes 11:2, "Divide your portion to seven, or even to eight, for you do not know what misfortune may occur on the earth."

Within five years Grace had improved her financial position to where she was able to give more than 50 percent of her earnings away and still have over $100,000 a year income.

One additional comment on Catherine's situation: She was able to recover about $100,000 of her investment capital with the planner through the brokerage house he represented. He lost his securities license and was barred from ever selling commodities again.

The pastor left the church and the new pastor accepted the financial obligation to Catherine seriously. Her loan was repaid in a little more than three years (without interest). Catherine recovered enough money to live a modest lifestyle, wiser and more cautious about her inheritance.

A prudent widow would do well to remember this cliché: "When in doubt, don't." Or as Proverbs 14:18 says, "The naive inherit folly, but the prudent are crowned with knowledge."

■ 9 WIDOWS WITHOUT AN INHERITANCE

It would be great if all widows could have at their disposal all the assets of Catherine and Grace, the two women mentioned in chapter 8. All that would be necessary would be to train them how to invest and manage the inheritance.

However, the majority of widows do not have large amounts of money available to them. Typically their husbands were employed in average income jobs, had a nominal amount of insurance ($25,000 to $50,000), and practically no assets except a home with a mortgage and a car with more debt than equity. For these single parents it means they must rely on Social Security and Dependent Care benefits. They must work and use their insurance money as a buffer until the children are grown. Generally they have a difficult time.

Eighty percent of the widows under the age of 50 will remarry within five years, creating a whole new set of decisions and possible conflicts. Should you have a prenuptial agreement for the funds from your first marriage? What if your husband has children too? Should your children's monthly benefits be held only for their care? These, and many other related questions, can best be answered on the basis of God's Word. But I'm getting ahead of myself. First, widows without assets.

The Case of Stacy
Stacy was 32 years old when her husband Tom first learned that he had cancer. Over the next two years they spent hundreds of thousands of dollars on medical treatments. Fortunately Tom had good insurance through his employer, but even so, they still had to pay the 20 percent deductible, up to $10,000 each year. This effectively depleted their reserves and forced them to sell their home for the equity.

When Tom died, two years after being diagnosed, they were down to living paycheck to paycheck. They had been members of a large Baptist church for several years and had many friends there who helped during the last dark hours when Tom was wasting away. They brought meals to the family and in the last few weeks several of the older ladies sat with Tom at the hospital in the evenings so that Stacy could get some rest. During that time several people asked Stacy about their finances but, in typical fashion for most people, she always responded, "We're making it OK." Usually that's where they left it after saying, "Well if you ever have a need, you call us." That's a pretty safe statement in our generation because our inherent pride will keep most of us from asking. It is only by consistent prodding that these barriers are broken down. It's not that most Christians don't care; they do. But they also don't want to feel pushy.

Tom had a total of $10,000 in life insurance. He had known that he needed more but funds were always tight and it wasn't a high priority for a man under 30. After he was diagnosed with cancer he was totally uninsurable. Guilt kept him from discussing it with Stacy, even though they both knew she would have a difficult time financially after his death trying to support their three children.

The insurance proceeds were sent almost immediately after the company received the death certificate from their insurance agent. Stacy paid the funeral bill of nearly $2,500 and some miscellaneous outstanding bills amounting to $1,200. She then deposited the remainder in her savings account to live on until she started receiving the Social Security checks.

Several weeks went by with no word from Social Security, during which time Stacy called the local office several times. All she could find out was that the claim had been filed and forwarded to the Washington office. Stacy then wrote a letter to the national headquarters telling them of her urgency.

A few days later she received a letter from the Social Security administration stating that there was a problem with her claim and giving her a number to call for further information. When she called the number she told the receptionist her name and was asked to hold on while her call was being transferred to a claims worker.

"Hello, Mrs. Johnston?" the case worker asked more as a statement than a question.

131

"Yes, this is Mrs. Johnston," Stacy replied.

"Mrs. Johnston, we seem to have a problem with your application for Social Security Survivor Benefits."

"What kind of problem?" Stacy asked. She could sense her heart speeding up in response to the comment.

"It seems that our records of your husband, Thomas, only go back to 1983. Did he work at a job that was exempt from Social Security assessment before that?"

"Why no, I'm sure he didn't. We've been married nearly 10 years now and Tom worked for two other firms, but they all paid into Social Security."

"There must be some kind of mix-up in the records then," the case worker said. "Have you ever requested an audit of your husband's Social Security account?"

"No, I didn't know I could."

"Yes. It's a service provided by the department. Unfortunately we aren't required to adjust any file beyond three years if a discrepancy occurs."

"What exactly does that mean?" Stacy asked as her anxiety level heightened more.

"It means that since your husband's account shows contributions only since 1983, your benefits will be greatly reduced."

Panic struck. "That simply can't be!" Stacy said desperately. "Tom paid in all those years, even before we were married. What can I do to get this straightened out?"

"I would suggest you write a letter to the district supervisor. Do you have any employment records for the years prior to 1983?"

"I'm not sure. Tom kept all the records."

"Well it might help if you had some evidence. You can get a copy of your income tax statements from the Internal Revenue Service. Although sometimes it takes several months to get the copies."

Several months, Stacy thought to herself. I don't have enough money to last several months.

After hanging up the phone Stacy ran to the basement to search the old file cabinet where Tom always kept their previous years' records. There, neatly labeled and banded with rubber bands, she found all the income tax statements dating back 15 years.

Praise the Lord for Tom, she thought as she looked over the records. Every withholding statement was attached and all of them reflected Social Security withholding for each year.

Stacy hurried to the local library where she made copies of all the withholding statements. She then wrote a letter to the Social Security district office, as instructed earlier. She mailed the letter the next morning and followed it up with a telephone call as soon as she thought enough time had passed for the letter to arrive.

"Mrs. Johnston, this is Mrs. Combs, the district supervisor for claims. We did receive your letter and the verification of Social Security withholding on your husband, Thomas. I will forward your request for reevaluation to our national office."

"You mean you can't approve my support?" Stacy said as she felt the fear rise again.

"No, I'm afraid not, Mrs. Johnston. That can only be done at the Social Security headquarters. By law, we are not bound to make adjustments after three years."

"But how can you do that?" Stacy cried. "We paid into the system all those years."

"I understand how you feel, Mrs. Johnston. But we didn't make the laws; Congress did. You'll have to wait until your appeal is heard."

Needless to say Stacy spent some sleepless nights waiting for a reply from the Social Security administration. In the meantime an attorney from her church called their congressman about Stacy's case. The congressman then called the Social Security office to check on her request. He was assured the department would do all they could to rectify the problem.

During this period Stacy discovered what Christian love is all about. When the members of the Sunday School class heard about her dilemma they took up a special offering to help her financially. The next four months she received anonymous gifts totaling nearly $3,000. The church was considering taking the family on as a missions project when she finally heard from the Social Security. The letter read:

Dear Mrs. Johnston:

Your request for reevaluation of Social Security Survivor's Benefits has been received and I'm glad to tell you that the benefits have been recalculated based on the records you provided. Enclosed is a check for the entire period during which you and your children were entitled.

Fortunately for Stacy and her children she was supported by a strong church family that was willing to obey God's Word. As James 2:14-16 says, "What use is it, my brethren, if a man says he has faith, but he has no works? Can that faith save him? If a brother or sister is without clothing and in need of daily food, and one of you says to them, 'Go in peace, be warmed and be filled,' and yet you do not give them what is necessary for their body, what use is that?" Stacy's life since she has been widowed has not been easy. But it would have been a much smoother transition had her husband decided to provide his family with enough insurance to meet their needs for at least a reasonable time period. Obviously God still provided, but I question if it was His best plan.

Many widows are faced with almost impossible circumstances because their husbands didn't plan properly and left them with virtually no assets. Often it is a misguided Christian who believes that having insurance is a lack of faith. Insurance can be used to an extreme and become the symbol of a lack of faith. But if used properly — to provide — it is good stewardship. If a couple has been prudent and they are able to save enough to meet the family's needs in the event of the husband's death, then insurance may no longer be necessary. But for most families it is a means of providing in the early, critical years when funds are tight and a surplus is difficult to accumulate.

Is Insurance Necessary?

Jerry Rice had been a successful building contractor most of his adult life and had provided well for his family. He and his wife Alice had three children, all of whom they helped put through college and were now living on their own.

Unfortunately, Jerry did not believe in insurance, considering it a waste of money. In their 35 years of marriage the largest medical expenses they had were the births of their children, which Jerry paid for out of his personal income. Then, at age 55, Jerry suffered his first heart attack. Two weeks later he had triple by-pass surgery. The bills amounted to nearly $60,000. Jerry and Alice were able to scrape up the money by mortgaging several pieces of property they owned. Jerry was forced to cut back on his work and their income dropped substantially. Over the next year Jerry continued to have recurring heart problems and ultimately was diagnosed with a severe infection that was destroying his heart muscle.

After several bouts with congestive heart failure and nearly three months of hospitalization, Jerry died leaving Alice with nearly $100,000 in additional medical expenses to repay.

After Jerry's death Alice began to sell off all their accumulated assets, including their home. She was able to pay off the majority of the outstanding debts but ended up with virtually no money. At 57 years of age Alice began to look for work.

She ultimately ended up working for a retreat center as their cook, making $600 a month. Unable to pay normal rent in her area she found a small trailer that she could afford. She also sold her newest car and ended up driving Jerry's work truck with over 100,000 miles on it.

I first met Alice while doing a conference at the retreat center. I was impressed by her humble spirit and uncomplaining nature. The camp director was concerned about her since he knew they were not really meeting all of her financial needs. He asked if I would talk with her and try to find out how she was doing on a month-in, month-out basis.

One evening after everyone else had left, I had a chance to talk with Alice.

"Alice, how did you come to work for the camp?" I asked.

"Oh, the Lord just led me here after my husband died," she said enthusiastically. "I really love it here. The people are so nice and I get to hear some good speakers. I believe these young couples need to hear what you have to say. Many of them are so deeply in debt that they can't serve the Lord. My husband Jerry and I never believed in borrowing if we could avoid it."

The conversation continued like this for several minutes until I had the chance to ask about her own finances.

"Alice, did Jerry leave you enough resources that you're able to take a job like this without being concerned about your monthly income?"

"No, unfortunately Jerry's illness took nearly everything we had," she responded without any hint of self-pity. "But God always provides and He gave me this job because He knew I needed to be around Christian people."

"What about your monthly expenses? Are you able to meet all your needs?"

"Sometimes it's real tight but we always learned to get along on what we made."

I asked if she would mind if we went over her monthly expenses and income, to which she responded, "No, that would be fine. But I don't want to take up your time."

I assured her that I was there for just that purpose and spent the next several minutes writing down her average monthly budget. I know her husband loved her and always thought he was providing as best he could. But if he had looked over the budget I saw, he would have cried. Alice had $25 every two weeks for food, $25 a month for all utilities, $10 a month for medical expenses, etc. She was trying to live on the equivalent of a utility bill for many families.

I asked if her children helped her with her monthly expenses, trying to determine if she had any outside source of income.

"No, I haven't discussed this with my children. They all have families of their own and I wouldn't want to be a burden to them."

"What about friends in your church?"

"I haven't really discussed my situation with anyone prior to this," she said. "I don't want to be a burden to anyone. The Lord will meet my needs."

"I believe that Alice," I told her. "But I also believe that the Lord uses people to do it. There are many strong admonitions to support widows, especially those of your own household as Paul said in 1 Timothy 5:16, 'If any woman who is a believer has dependent widows, let her assist them, and let not the church be burdened, so that it may assist those who are widows indeed.' Perhaps you have denied your children and friends the right to help by not telling them."

"Why, I never thought about that," Alice said as she continued to stack the dishes.

Before I left we agreed that she would contact her children and let them know about her situation. Then based on their response, she would decide whether she should let her friends at church know. Unknown to either of us at that time one of her friends had already taken her case to the pastor. He agreed to help out of the benevolence fund, enough to pay her utility bills. In addition, one of the members who was an air conditioning contractor volunteered to install an air conditioner in her trailer so that it would be livable in the summer months.

Later I found out that Alice had written each of her children a note simply stating that she was having some temporary financial problems. Her oldest daughter called immediately and asked her the extent of the problems. When she learned that her mother had sold their home and virtually all her possessions to pay bills, she contacted the other two children about helping. Within a month they were providing $300 a month to their mother. Along with the church's help, Alice was able to live in reasonable comfort, and actually save a little for the future. Eventually she was relocated into a cottage on the retreat center property and her situation improved considerably. God's people provided where her husband had been negligent. Unfortunately, not all widows in similar circumstances are so fortunate.

More information on how to decide your life insurance needs can be found in Appendix E. Even if your personal needs are now met, you may have children or friends who can benefit from this information.

Words of Counsel

If I could offer one piece of counsel to widows who find themselves without an inheritance it would be: *Let the other Christians around you know that you have needs — and be specific.* Almost without exception the believers who know about a widow's needs will respond and help. The thing that keeps most widows from letting their needs be known is *pride!*

Your responsibility as a widow in need is to pare down your cost of living to where it is "reasonable." What is reasonable? This is often hard to define, but think of what you would expect of a widow you might be counseling who needed your support. You certainly don't need to live impoverished, nor do you need to trim all comforts out of your life. What is expected is a reasonable, balanced lifestyle. But then, that's really no different than God's plan for all of us.

I would suggest seeking out a good financial counselor in your area to help you develop a budget. The budget should generally conform to the model found in Appendix A of this book. Every category must be funded or your budget won't work long-term. That means surplus funds for car replacement, clothes, insurance, vacations, etc. These are all a part of our society and there is nothing wrong with them if kept in balance.

■ 10 WHAT EVERY WIDOW NEEDS TO KNOW ABOUT WILLS, TRUSTS, INSURANCE, SOCIAL SECURITY, AND TAXES

Perhaps the most depressing and frustrating situation for any widow is dealing with the decisions she has to make after the death of a spouse. Most widows would willingly turn all the decisions over to someone else so they wouldn't have to think about them. Unfortunately, except in rare instances, no one else is able to deal with most of these issues. Others can help by contacting the various agencies — such as Social Security, the Veterans' Administration, and the Internal Revenue Service — necessary to complete the transfer of assets and secure future income. But rarely will anyone else have the details necessary to complete the transactions. Also it is vital for any widow to understand the process. Otherwise, you will always feel like you're dependent on someone else to make your decisions.

In this section I will explain many of the options that are available, as well as the forms that need to be ordered. Hopefully this will remove some of the mystery and will provide enough information for a concerned loved one to help. In the event that you need to refer to this information later, I have included a summary in Appendix C for quick reference. Also included in Appendix J are some forms that will help to keep the necessary information organized. If you decide to use them, I would suggest taking them to a quick copy printer and having them expanded to fit a standard 8½" x 11" notebook.

Probate

The term *probate* means to prove, or to testify. When a will is probated it is "proved" before the judge in the court of the ordinary (in most states). To be valid a will must conform to the requirements of the state in which it is to be proved. These requirements vary state by state and a will drafted according to the laws in one state may not be probatable in another. Some states require one witness on a will; others require two or more. Some states require that all immediate heirs be named in the will, regardless of whether or not they receive an inheritance; others do not. So it is very important that a will be reviewed by an attorney or competent adviser who is familiar with laws of your state.

Probating a will is not particularly complicated and does not generally require an attorney. The exception would be where there is a question about its validity, or there is a challenge to it by an heir, thus requiring a legal defense. To probate a will you must deliver the original copy to the recorder at the court of the ordinary. Your probate hearing will be put on the court calendar and will usually be reviewed within 30 days (depending on the court load). If there are no irregularities in the document, the court will approve it and the will becomes public record.

The judge will assign the executor named in the will to have the estate appraised, if necessary, and the assets distributed as specified in the will. The executor will report back to the court when all the terms of the will have been completed.

There is a cost to probate a will in most states. These costs vary greatly, depending on the state. Future probate costs can be avoided by the use of trusts. These will be discussed a little later.

The Executor's Duties

An executor (executrix) can be named by the deceased in his or her will. If one is not named, or those named cannot serve, the court will assign an executor. The duties of an executor are to literally "execute" the terms of the will. These include probating the will, locating the heirs and beneficiaries, preparing the necessary property evaluations, paying the estate and inheritance taxes, if any, and distributing the assets to the named beneficiaries.

A single executor may be named, or multiple executors who will work as a team. Anyone may be named as executor, including beneficiaries, friends, relatives, attorneys, or accountants.

The court will allow the executor to receive reasonable

compensation for the services performed unless specifically prohibited in the will. Out-of-state executors may be required to post bonds matching the total estate value unless that requirement is waived by the will.

An executor(s) is a fiduciary (legally accountable), and as such, can perform only within the confines of the deceased's will. An executor can be held liable for any misdistribution or misuse of assets while performing as executor. In other words, an executor cannot arbitrarily distribute assets to anyone unless specified by the will.

Inheritance and Death Taxes

All estates are potentially taxable upon the death of the owner. There are two types of taxes: federal estate taxes and state death taxes. Whether or not an estate incurs these taxes depends on the estate size and the ultimate beneficiaries. This presentation is not meant to be an exhaustive study on this subject and if you have any questions about your estate, I would highly recommend seeing a competent estate planning attorney in your area.

• *Federal Estate Taxes*

SPOUSAL INHERITANCE. A spouse can receive an unlimited amount of assets through inheritance without incurring any federal estate taxes. The marital deduction exemption is meant to allow a spouse to receive these assets to live on without dilution. However, upon the death of both spouses the assets of the estate will be subject to federal estate taxes.

OTHER BENEFICIARIES. Anyone, other than a surviving spouse, who is a beneficiary of an estate can receive up to $600,000 in assets without incurring federal estate taxes. This is a cumulative total of all assets distributed to all the beneficiaries. Above this amount the estate is subject to a progressive federal estate tax of up to 49 percent. Appendix H shows a chart of the federal estate tax table.

All gifts from one person to another above $10,000 per year per donor ($20,000 for a couple) are subject to gift taxes. The gift taxes paid represent a credit against potential estate taxes. However, if the gift taxes were not paid in the year of transfer, these assets are potentially taxable in the estate.

Good estate planning is essential for any surviving spouse with total assets exceeding $600,000 fair market value. Otherwise the assets can be severely diluted through estate and death taxes when you die. It would be far better stewardship to leave those assets to the Lord's work than donate them involuntarily to the government.

In summary, a spouse can receive an unlimited estate without incurring federal estate taxes. Other beneficiaries can receive up to $600,000 in property before incurring federal estate taxes. Previous gifts in excess of the exempt amount ($10,000 per person) on which gift taxes have been paid are credited against any federal estate taxes.

- *State Death Taxes*

Although the Federal Estate tax code exempts all assets left to a spouse and up to $600,000 left to other beneficiaries, the same is not necessarily true of state death taxes. Many states have adopted the same code as the federal government, but several have not. If you happen to live in one of the states that tax a widow's inheritance, the financial shock can be severe. Many couples have actually changed their state of primary residence just for this reason.

Appendix I shows the state death tax table as of January 1990. These can change as time passes. If you have a question about the taxes in your state I would suggest contacting your state Tax Commissioner's office. They will provide you with a current tax table. Remember that state death taxes are also graduated, and as such, will increase as the estate grows. This is particularly important for you as a widow leaving assets to your beneficiaries. Each year you can gift up to $10,000 per person without incurring any gift taxes. Often this is a good planning tool to reduce the eventual estate tax impact. Also remember that any assets left to a nonprofit organization are exempt from federal and state taxes.

Wills

If you are a widow and your husband didn't leave a will, it's obviously too late to correct that error. However, you can correct your own situation by having a will made that prescribes the distribution of your current assets. The cost of having a will made is slight compared to the cost of not having one if you die.

The question is often asked, "Can I draw up my own will, or do I need an attorney?" Anyone can draw her own will. It's called a holographic will (self-made). You need to be sure that it conforms to the laws of your state, including the proper number of witnesses. However, most good counselors don't recommend that people try to draft their own wills. If you do it wrong, it's too late to correct it after you die. To have an attorney review your holographic will would probably cost almost as much as having him draft one.

There are "will kit" books available in most bookstores. Generally these are accurate and provide enough information for a layman to draft his or her own will. But remember, most often the judge reviewing a will is an attorney. Any flaw in the will can invalidate the entire document. For any potentially taxable estate it's just not worth the risk, in my opinion.

If you have a simple estate situation and are willing to shop around a little bit, you can probably find an attorney who will draft your will for less than $200. Don't hesitate to ask any attorney you call what he or she charges before you commit to having the will made. I assure you they don't hesitate to ask the price of a car they're buying—the principle is the same.

Before having a will drafted you need to write out exactly what you want done with your assets after you die. If you have assets that you want left to specific individuals, you need to be very explicit. Later if the circumstances change or you change your mind, you can modify your will with a codicil (amendment). You *don't* have to create a new will.

If you have previous wills in existence, you need to specify that your latest will supersedes all previous wills so the judge won't think you were simply adding to an existing document.

The original copy of your will should be kept in a safe location. Without it, probating your will would be difficult or impossible. I suggest it be kept at your accountant's or attorney's office with a note in your home files about where the will is located. Many people lock the original in their safety deposit box. But unless another person is authorized to enter the box, it would take a court order to open it after your death. This can delay the probate process several weeks or even months. If no one knows about the safety deposit box, it might be impossible to locate the will.

If you own property in two or more states, it can be controlled by the will probated in your primary residence state. However, you need to clearly identify all properties in a statement attached to your will, and you must still pay any taxes due in that other state(s).

Trusts

Trusts are becoming increasingly popular since they eliminate the need for probating any properties held in the trust. Also, a trust can assure more confidentiality than a will. A trust document can be viewed as a contract to manage assets for you. You can make this contract effective during your lifetime, in which case it is called an inter-vivos or living trust. Or you can make it effective after your death only, in which case it is called a testamentary (after death) trust. Usually these are created within your will and activated when the will is probated.

There are two kinds of living trusts: revocable and irrevocable. Assets placed in an irrevocable trust are the property of the trust and cannot be recovered. Those placed in a revocable trust can be changed or removed as you desire. A revocable trust obviously becomes irrevocable upon the death of the donor to the trust.

Both the revocable and irrevocable trusts eliminate the need to probate assets assigned to them. However, since the donor has the right to remove any assets assigned to a revocable trust, they are treated as estate assets and are subject to estate or death taxes as previously discussed.

Assets assigned to an irrevocable trust cease to be the property of the donor (grantor) and are removed from the estate. However, they are still subject to the same rules for gifted properties previously discussed.

If you reserve an interest in the assets assigned to an irrevocable trust, such as a life estate (the right to live there) or a lifetime income, then a portion of the assets can be valued in the estate and subject to taxation. A professional attorney is needed to evaluate the assets and liabilities of trusts.

Charitable Trusts

Charitable trusts are increasingly popular among Christian widows, and as such, deserve a brief evaluation. These trusts are often called charitable remainder trusts because the residual in the trust, upon the death of the donor, must go to a qualified charitable organization. The donor reserves a lifetime income from the assets assigned to the trust, which is usually managed by the charitable beneficiary. Because a portion of the assets will eventually go to the charity (one or more), the donor is allowed a current charitable deduction from income taxes at the time of assignment to the trust. This amount is calculated by the IRS on the basis of how much benefit the donor receives during his or her lifetime versus how much the charity will eventually receive. Obviously, the assets remaining in the trust at the time of the donor's death are not subject to taxation.

Gift Annuities

A gift annuity works much the same as a charitable remainder trust in that the donor assigns assets (usually cash or marketable securities) in exchange for a lifetime income, or annuity. The donor is allowed a current charitable deduction on his or her income taxes based on the remainder value that the charity will receive. The primary difference between the charitable remainder trust and the gift annuity is that the donor is guaranteed the income from a charitable remainder trust only as long as there are available assets earning income. If the assets are depleted, the income stops.

In a gift annuity the income is guaranteed for as long as the donor lives, regardless of whether the assets are depleted or not. Usually the percentages of guaranteed income from a gift annuity will be less than that from a charitable trust. The logic of this is obvious — contingent liability on the part of the charity.

Social Security Benefits

Dependent survivors of Social Security participants are entitled to some financial benefits up to age 18. The surviving spouse can also draw benefits for the care of dependent children. The amount of benefits available is calculated on the amount the deceased paid into the system during his or her lifetime. To be fully insured (vested), a worker must have paid in at least 40 quarters at the highest rate. Fewer quarters of participation or lower pay-in will reduce the amount of the benefits paid.

To determine how much benefits are available you will need to contact the local Social Security Administration office or file a copy of form SSA-7004 with the Social Security department. A sample copy of this form is provided in Appendix C.

If you are a widow caring for dependent children and relying on survivors' benefits, you will need to be doing some financial planning prior to your children reaching age 16 unless one or more of them is permanently disabled. Although *their* benefits will continue until age 18 (or age 19 if they are still in high school), *your* benefits will cease when the youngest child reaches age 16. You may also qualify for survivors' retirement benefits, but they will not start until age 60 (except for disability).

You need to apply for Social Security benefits as soon as possible after the death of your spouse. To do so you need to contact your local Social Security office and supply a copy of the deceased's death certificate, your proof of marriage, and your children's birth certificates. The benefits paid are based on a complex table used by Social Security, but basically you can expect about one-half of your spouse's average earnings over the last five years if he was fully vested.

BURIAL BENEFITS. Social Security will also pay a one-time

$225 lump sum to help with burial expenses. You need only show proof of death to receive this benefit.

DISABILITY BENEFITS. As the spouse of a fully insured participant, you and your dependents may qualify for disability benefits. Unlike survivors' or retirement benefits, disability payments are not dependent on the age of the recipients.

RETIREMENT BENEFITS. Perhaps the best known element of Social Security is the old age or so-called retirement benefit. To be eligible for retirement benefits you must meet the qualifications of the program. Presently that is 40 quarters of contributions into the system. Under certain conditions spouses of deceased participants who qualify may also draw benefits from their spouses' contributions. To determine your benefits it is necessary to contact the Social Security Administration office in your area. Appendix C contains a table showing the approximate benefits as of 1990.

VETERAN'S BENEFITS. Surviving spouses of Armed Service veterans who die in the service of their country may qualify for benefits, as may their dependents. These benefits, known as Dependency and Indemnity Compensation (DIC) are intended to help widows and dependents of veterans. Originally they were limited to service-related deaths, but coverage has been extended to include those who were disabled from a service-related cause but whose death was not service-related. To determine if you or your children qualify for these benefits you should contact the Veterans' Administration in Washington, D.C. The address and further information is provided in Appendix D.

Health Insurance

One factor often overlooked in the death of a spouse is the fact that the family's health insurance may be lost if it was through a group plan at the husband's place of employment. By federal law the employer must offer the surviving dependents the option of continuing the health insurance at the same rate the company pays for 18 months after his (or her) death (the so-called C.O.B.R.A. Act). Beyond that time, the insurance company may elect to extend the policy but the rate will normally be based on an individual policy premium. Also they may not cover existing medical conditions at the time of changeover.

There are few options other than the high costs of individual health insurance plans. One option is to purchase a major medical plan. The intent of a major medical policy is to cover the catastrophic expenses of a major health problem. Often the deductible minimum may be $1,000 to $5,000. The cost of this type of health policy may be one-half to one-third of a more typical health plan with a $100 to $500 deductible.

For those who cannot afford the cost of a health or major medical policy, a unique alternative may be found in associations that self-insure their members. One such plan is the Brotherhood Association previously mentioned in chapter 7. This association accepts only professing Christians who are nonsmokers and nondrinkers. Each month the association divides the medical expenses incurred by its members and each participant pays a proportionate share. If you cannot afford the cost of medical insurance, I would encourage you to investigate this plan.

Life Insurance
Often the question is asked, "Should I carry life insurance on myself and the children now that I am a widow?"

The issue of insurance of any kind is relatively simple: *Insurance should only be used to provide—never to profit or protect.* The Lord should be our protection, and profiting should be a strategy of an investment plan, not an insurance plan.

If your husband left sufficient assets to provide for you and your family upon his death, you may have no further need for additional insurance. If, however, he failed to provide adequately you may want to supplement your provision to your children through additional insurance in the event of your untimely death. Appendix E contains a summary of how to calculate how much life insurance you may need, as well as what type of insurance may best suit your needs and budget.

In my opinion there is virtually no real need for insurance

on minor children, despite the two usual arguments for doing so. The first is that it assures their future insurability. Since the vast majority of 18- to 21-year-old adults are insurable, this would not seem to be a large risk. If funds are limited, it would be a much better use of the money to put it into current needs or save it in higher earning investments for things like education.

The second common reason presented for insurance on minor children is to cover the costs of burial expenses in the event of a tragedy. Although this is a valid reason, I believe there is a less costly way to provide for this contingency. There is a nonprofit association called the "Memorial Society" that functions in most of the United States, offering low-cost burial coverage. The address for the national organization is: Continential Association of Funeral and Memorial Societies, Inc., 7910 Woodmont Avenue, Suite 1208, Bethesda, Maryland 20814. If you are interested, write and ask for a brochure and the nearest local chapter.

■ 11 REMARRIAGE DECISIONS

Nearly 90 percent of all widows will get remarried. You may not think you will right now, but time has a way of healing many wounds and reviving old feelings. There is no reason why a widow should not get remarried, assuming it is the Lord's will. According to the Apostle Paul in 1 Timothy 5:14, "Therefore, I want younger widows to get married, bear children, keep house, and give the enemy no occasion for reproach." Often that is sound advice for older widows as well. Solomon said in Ecclesiastes 4:9-10, "Two are better than one because they have a good return for their labor. For if either of them falls, the one will lift up his companion. But woe to the one who falls when there is not another to lift him up." God designed us to live in pairs, with few exceptions.

Remarriage for the widow with children brings with it a whole new set of decisions, and sometimes problems. I would like to discuss some of the more common of these.

Prenuptial Agreements

Agreements between two people contemplating marriage are becoming more common in a society that plans for divorce before the marriage begins. Unfortunately, many of these people are Christians who have been deceived by the world around them into believing that they must protect their assets against a future spouse. To do this merely allows Satan a foothold in the marriage that he will exercise at his leisure.

There are some circumstances where a prenuptial agreement may be biblical, as well as logical, and we will examine these. But for the most part, they drive a wedge in a relationship that will quickly turn into a rift, under the right set of conditions.

My Stuff, Your Stuff

One example I recall vividly was that of Jan and Mike. Jan had lost her husband three years earlier through an automobile accident. Mike had lost his wife two years earlier after a long struggle with diabetes.

Jan had received a settlement of nearly $500,000 from the death of her husband. This, along with $200,000 in life insurance proceeds, provided her a comfortable living. Mike, on the other hand, had been a missionary when his wife was diagnosed with diabetes and had returned to the States to seek treatment. During the intervening five years he had worked as interim pastor for several churches, just barely scraping by and accumulating some sizable medical bills.

They met at a church missions conference where Mike was a guest speaker. His message was on the time he had spent in the jungles of Central America. Jan was so impressed by his humility and gentle spirit that she asked him home for dinner one evening.

Their relationship developed over the next several months with neither of them discussing their financial situations. It was obvious though that Jan lived comfortably and Mike, very frugally. They freely discussed their previous spouses and how difficult the transition had been to single life again. Within a year Mike had proposed to Jan and she accepted.

When she told her children about the pending marriage, they hit the ceiling. We'll pick up the discussion at this point as Jan talks with her oldest daughter, Megan.

"Mother, you hardly know this man," she said sharply. "How do you know he's not just out after your money?"

"Mike's not like that, honey. He has never mentioned money to me."

"Sure, but he can see you're pretty well off though," Megan said caustically. "That money was provided by Daddy and I don't think it's right that some stranger should get it if something happens to you. You need a prenuptial agreement, so if the marriage doesn't last or you die, the money will go to us kids."

"I don't know if that's a good idea. Mike might think I don't trust him," Jan said as she thought about how such an agreement might affect Mike.

"So what? If he's really not after your money, he won't mind. If he does, you'll know he's a phony."

After several similar conversations with her other children

Jan decided she should talk it over with Mike.

"Mike, my children think we should have an agreement about the money that came from my husband's death. They feel it should go to them if something happened to me," Jan said sheepishly as they sat in her living room.

"I agree totally," Mike said. "That money belongs to your family. I wouldn't want it no matter what. God has always provided for me and He still will."

"Are you sure you won't resent it if we have a prenuptial agreement then?"

"Absolutely not, Jan. I wouldn't want to do anything that might jeopardize your relationship with your family."

Jan had the agreement drawn by her son-in-law, who was a practicing attorney. It was very explicit that whatever assets were brought into the marriage by either party would be passed to the heirs upon the death of that person. The document went on to require an accounting of all assets and liabilities just prior to the marriage by an independent accounting firm.

Mike signed the agreement even though inside he knew that the very concept of a prenuptial agreement was wrong. If the circumstances had been reversed, his decision would have been absolute; he would never have held his assets away from Jan. But because he was basically broke and Jan had the assets, he felt that to say anything would be viewed as covetousness on his part.

Jan had the same basic feelings about the agreement, but hesitated to voice her feelings because of the pressure from the children. This was amplified even further when they saw the accounting of their estates. It was clear that Mike owned virtually nothing and, in fact, owed nearly $40,000 from previous medical bills.

Based on this new information, the children began to put pressure on their mother to further stipulate that none of her assets could be used to pay Mike's bills. She struggled with this new restriction, but finally caved in to their insistent pressure.

After Jan shared once more with Mike how her children

felt, he said, "Jan, no relationship can be built on anything other than mutual trust and dependence on God's Word. I don't seek or desire anything you have, but I also cannot be anything less than the head of my own household and still be worthy of teaching others. I believe it would be best if we call off our wedding. I wouldn't want your children, or you, to ever feel I had taken advantage of your material wealth. But I would rather remain single than feel that we are less than one."

"But Mike, I love you," Jan said as she realized that he was serious about dissolving their relationship. She began to realize what Mike said was right and her children were reacting from totally selfish motives.

"I love you too, Jan," Mike said honestly. "But I love the Lord first and foremost, and I believe God has given me this test to determine if I would compromise what I know to be right just to keep peace in your family. Remember what our Lord said in Luke 11:17, 'Any kingdom divided against itself is laid waste; and a house divided against itself falls.' "

For the next several weeks Jan did not hear from Mike, though when she saw him in church he was pleasant and courteous. As time passed she realized that he would not change his mind. She spent many fitful nights wondering if she had missed the Lord's direction in her life.

Several months later she learned that a Christian businessman in their church had paid all of Mike's medical bills so that he could return to the mission field. He was gone nearly three years before she saw him again. She was absolutely determined to ask his forgiveness for her doubting attitude and had written several times inquiring about him. Each time he had responded with a polite, but "arm's length" answer.

When at last he returned from the mission field Jan was devastated to learn that he had recently been married to a missionary's widow he had met in Central America. She had learned a lesson about conforming to this world's image rather than to God's—the hard way.

In Genesis 2:24 we see the example of the only perfect marriage between a man and a woman in all the Bible. It is

Adam and Eve before sin came into their lives, and here it is ordained, "For this cause man shall leave his father and his mother, and shall cleave to his wife; and they shall become one flesh." The Lord confirmed this relationship in Matthew 19:6, "Consequently they are no more two, but one flesh. What therefore God has joined together, let no man separate." God desires that a husband and wife be one working unit, literally one person. How can two be one when they divide their assets into two parts from the beginning? The material things are not the problem. They are merely the outside indicator of inside problems. As the Lord said in Luke 16:10, "He who is faithful in a very little thing is faithful also in much; and he who is unrighteous in a very little thing is unrighteous also in much."

I have counseled several couples who had prenuptial agreements. As best I know, none of them were benefited by the agreement and most were divided by it. More commonly it is a woman bringing assets into a second marriage who seeks a prenuptial agreement. Usually this is the result of a bitter experience from a first marriage, or bad counsel from those around her. Obviously we see many prenuptial agreements in the secular world as celebrities trade marriage partners as easily as most people trade automobiles. These relationships rarely last more than a few months, or years at best, and often still end up in bitter court battles. They must never be the pattern for Christian relationships.

When Is a Prenuptial Agreement Acceptable?

Where an older couple get married and neither has need for the finances of the other, an agreement can be made that all the assets will be held in trust for the lifetime of either surviving spouse. If the funds are not needed, the trust will be distributed to the heirs of the first spouse upon the death of the second. This effectively gives a couple total access to the funds if needed. But if they are not needed, the heirs are guaranteed the residual assets.

In this example there is no violation of the biblical principle of oneness. The assets would be available, but are held in reserve unless needed. I have seen this type of prenuptial agreement used quite effectively many times. Often it is not what the heirs might want for themselves, but it does assure the financial support of the surviving spouse without diverting one spouse's assets to the other's offspring.

His Kids, My Kids, Our Kids?

When two people who both have younger children get married, the situation can get very complicated when it comes to asset distribution. Often this is a source of potential conflict within the families. It is even more complicated when the wife brings considerable assets into the marriage that were provided by her first husband's family. The ex-husband's family often wants to maintain some control over the assets, even though they were given without reservation initially.

Jody was a widow with two children whose husband, Ken, had died in a boating accident. Ken's family had provided the funds for their home and a sizable trust fund for their family. The trust in Ken's name was payable to his widow (Jody), and the trusts for their two children were under her control, though stipulated for the education and support of his children only.

Jody had been a widow for nearly three years when she met John, a widower with two children, through their church single parents' group. After dating for several months they decided to get married. Ken's mother was extremely agitated with Jody's decision. John was a teacher and had virtually no assets other than a salary. Ken's mother, Pearl, didn't appreciate the idea that John would be benefiting from Ken's trust.

"I want you to guarantee me that the income from Ken's trust won't be used to support that man!" Pearl said in an irritated manner, as they sat having lunch at her club.

"I can't do that, Mother Hayes," Jody said politely. "John will be my husband and the father to Ken's children too. I can't keep my finances separate from his."

"He is not the father of my son's children," Pearl protested as she threw her napkin down on her plate. She was not used to people contradicting her.

"I know he's not their father. Ken was. But Ken is gone now and I want to get on with my life. John's a good and honest man who will love all of our children."

"He's a leech who knows a good deal when he sees it," Pearl said callously. "I'd like to see him support two families on his income."

"But Mother Hayes, the Lord has made it possible for us to combine families. I know it is through your generosity to Ken and your grandchildren but, after all, it all belongs to the Lord."

"I still don't want my money used to support some deadbeat," Pearl almost shouted. She always got angry when Jody tried to spiritualize everything that happened. Even when Ken drowned, she didn't hurt like I did, Pearl thought to herself.

"Mother Hayes, I will be glad to assign the trust back to you, as I have offered before."

"No, you can't do that! Then you'll have my grandchildren living in poverty too. I won't have that." Besides, Pearl knew that her husband, Ken Sr., would not allow the trust to be returned. He had often said, "Pearl, you need to let go and allow Jody to live her own life. You can't use our money to manipulate her and the kids."

"Then you will have to allow me to decide how the funds will be used," Jody replied respectfully. "When John is my husband we will share all things in common. Ken would have wanted it that way too."

Sure, because he was brainwashed by that church they went to, Pearl thought. Ever since he got religion, I lost him as a son. He could have run his father's business one day and married a girl his equal. Instead he became a campus minister and married someone whose father was a truck driver.

After Jody and John were married, Pearl continued her attacks, only now directed at John. She never failed to remind him that he was living on her money and was little more than a leech as far as she was concerned. Whenever she would have the grandchildren over for a visit, they would become belligerent for weeks upon their return home. Often they would echo their grandmother's sentiments. When John would give them directions, they would reply, "You're not our father. We don't have to do what you say. Grandmother Hayes told us so."

Finally in exasperation John and Jody confronted Pearl. "Mrs. Hayes," John said as they stood in her library, "I know that you don't approve of Jody's remarriage. But she and I are one and we're trying to do the best by all the children. Jody is going to have another child and we want all the children to accept each other as equals."

Pearl interrupted, "Ken's children will have the best that money can provide. They can afford to go to the best schools."

"That's true," John agreed. "But for right now they're just children who need the love and discipline of their parents. Jody and I have decided that we will no longer use any of the funds from Ken's trust. Also we will not allow the children to draw any funds from their trust, except for college, which is a long way off."

"I won't have it!" Pearl said bitterly. "I will not have my grandchildren living like paupers. You don't make enough money to provide for your family."

"Perhaps not by your standards, Mrs. Hayes. But Jody and I have worked out a budget that will allow us to make it. And I have begun to sell some articles to some magazines. We will make it."

"Well I won't allow it!" Pearl shouted as her husband, Ken Sr., came into the room.

"Won't allow what?" Ken Hayes asked.

"They seem to think they can get by on his salary," Pearl said, fuming. "And they said they won't allow the grandchildren to use their trust money either."

"Good for you," Ken said to John and Jody. "A little suffering will do those kids good. Pearl seems to forget that we didn't inherit our money; I earned it. And we had some tough times early on. I believe it helped to build the character I saw in Ken Jr. as a young man. He never was impressed with money, and did what he believed was the right thing to do."

The next four or five years were times of financial struggle for John and Jody, as well as all their children. But as John's income improved through his writing, they were able to buy a home. Throughout their grammar school and high school days the boys all slept in one bedroom, the girls in another. They grew close as a family and John's persistent loving attitude won over Ken's children. As they grew into teenagers they read some of their father's notes on his ministry work and realized how little he counted material success as important.

This was one family that overcame the troubles of "his and her" kids, but only because their strength was firmly rooted in the Lord. Without that, and without Jody's total commitment to honoring her husband, their path might have been significantly different; as were those of other couples I have counseled.

The Story of Steve and Lucy

Steve was a federal employee who met Lucy shortly after the death of her husband, a Miami surgeon. Lucy came out of a wealthy family and had married into the "right" side of society. After meeting Steve, her mother flatly pronounced him to be inferior to their blood line and told Lucy as much. Lucy rejected her mother's evaluation, and against her objections, married Steve.

A position with a small firm opened up in the Miami area and Lucy convinced Steve to leave his secure government job and take it so that he would not have to travel as much. In the meantime they had moved into the home provided by her mother and were relying heavily on her trust income to meet the expenses of the home and education of Lucy's first two children.

Steve accepted the position with the Miami firm, run by a friend of Lucy's mother. Shortly thereafter, the firm eliminated the position and Steve found himself unemployed at age 40. Though trained as an accountant, he was unable to secure another position in the Miami area. He often said that it was the result of Lucy's very influential mother blackballing him with most of the major employers in the area. It appeared she had set up the situation with Steve to ensure that he would have to leave the area.

What Lucy's mother had not counted on was that Lucy would also leave, which she did. Steve secured a job in another state and he and Lucy moved there. Lucy made an honest effort to live on Steve's meager salary, but a life of luxury had modified her habits to where she could not clean her own house, cook their meals, or even dress her children.

When Lucy got pregnant she appealed to her mother for help, over Steve's objections. Within a month Lucy's mother had bought them a new home, hired full-time maid services, and paid for the best boarding schools for her grandchildren. Needless to say, Steve's self-esteem was at an all-time low. Lucy's mother continually cut Steve down in front of her daughter and grandchildren and announced that Thanksgiving that he would no longer be welcome at their traditional dinner. The same applied to both Christmas and New Year's. Since these holidays had always been spent at Grandma's house, the children were committed to going.

The first year Lucy stayed home with Steve. But as the years rolled by, she drifted more and more under the influence of her mother. As Steve and Lucy's child grew up, the grandmother alienated her from Steve as much as possible. The strain between the two families grew almost unbearable and Steve began to vent his frustration on Lucy. Eventually Lucy began to divide her time between her home with Steve and the home maintained by her mother in Miami. Steve's salary of $30,000 a year would hardly have paid the airfares for Lucy and the children to fly back and forth.

Then Lucy became very ill with an undiagnosed problem that left her partially paralyzed for several months. Instead of allowing Steve to care for her and the children, she packed up and moved to their home in Miami. While there, her mother convinced her that she should file for a legal separation from Steve, which she did. The sad side of this whole episode is that under normal circumstances Steve and Lucy could have had a good life together. But the tug of riches and an easier life overwhelmed Lucy and she could not do what she knew was God's will. Now, nearly 10 years later, Steve and Lucy are still legally separated and, unknown to Lucy, her mother has found a judge who issued a restraining order against Steve even seeing his own child. Lucy is dying of an inoperable brain tumor and her mother has been appointed her legal guardian as well as the children's. It is as the Apostle Paul wrote in 1 Timothy 6:10, "For the love of money is a root of all sorts of evil, and some by longing for it have wandered away from the faith, and pierced themselves with many a pang."

I sincerely pray that as you conclude this book God will give you the wisdom to become the best steward possible over the assets He has entrusted to you, both material and human. As a single parent, widowed or divorced, you need to allow those around you to help. Don't let pride keep you from letting your needs be known. If, for any reason, you don't get a biblical response from fellow believers, decide to help make some changes. Remember, there is no one better equipped to help single parents more than a single parent. As you give, you'll find God will provide—both time and resources.

Take the Lord at His Word and invest some of yourself in others. "Give, and it will be given to you; good measure, pressed down, shaken together, running over, they will pour into your lap. For whatever measure you deal out to others, it will be dealt to you in return" (Luke 6:38).

APPENDIX A

The following material is provided as a practical guide to help you establish a budget. It is not a detailed instruction on budgeting. For more information, ask your local bookstore for a copy of *The Financial Planning Workbook* published by Moody Press.

STEPS TO MAKING A BUDGET

In making and using a budget, there are several logical steps, each requiring individual effort. A sample form for budgeting is shown in Figure B (pages 169-70). Use this form to guide your budget preparation.

STEP 1 — List Expenditures in the Home on a Monthly Basis.

A. Fixed Expenses — These include the following:
   Tithe
   Federal income taxes (if taxes are deducted, ignore this item)
   State income taxes (if taxes are deducted, ignore this item)
   Federal Social Security taxes (if taxes are deducted, ignore this item)
   Housing expenses (payment/rent)
   Residence taxes
   Residence insurance
   Other

B. Variable Expenses:
   Food
   Outstanding debts
   Utilities
   Insurance (life, health, auto)
   Entertainment, recreation
   Clothing allowance
   Medical, dental

161

Savings
Miscellaneous

Note: In order to accurately determine variable expenses, it is suggested that you keep an expense diary for 30 days. List every expenditure, even small purchases.

STEP 2 – List Available Income per Month.

Note: If you operate on a non-fixed monthly income, use a yearly average divided into months.

Salary
Rents
Notes
Interest
Dividends
Income tax refund
Other

STEP 3 – Compare Income vs. Expenses.

If total income exceeds total expenses, you have only to implement a method of budget control in your home. If, however, expenses exceed income (or more stringent controls in spending are desired), additional steps are necessary. In that case, an analysis of each budget area is called for to reduce expenses.

BUDGET PROBLEM AREAS

BOOKKEEPING ERRORS

An accurately balanced checkbook is a must. Even small errors result in big problems if they are allowed to compound.

An inaccurate balance can result in an overdrawn account, as well as in significant bank charges.

Automatic banking systems create additional pitfalls. Automatic payment deductions must be subtracted from the checkbook ledger at the time they are paid by the bank.

EXAMPLE: An insurance premium is paid by automatic withdrawal on the fifteenth of each month. Since no statement or notice is received from the insurance company, you must make certain that on the fifteenth of every month the proper amount is deducted from your home checking account records.

The same would be true for automatic credit card payments or any other automatic withdrawal.

Direct deposits into checking accounts must also be noted in the home ledger at the proper time. *Don't forget* to include bank service charges in the home ledger.

Automatic Tellers: If you withdraw cash from your account using an outside/automatic teller, be sure you write it in your ledger and file the transaction record.

FACTORS IN KEEPING GOOD RECORDS

1. *Use a ledger type checkbook rather than a stub type.* The ledger gives greater visibility and lends itself to fewer errors. I usually recommend using a checkbook that has a copy of the checks written. This eliminates errors in not posting a check.

2. *Make certain all checks are accounted for.* All checks should be entered in the ledger when written. This entry

must include the check number, amount, date, and assignee.

Tearing checks out of your checkbook for future use defeats many of the safeguards built into this system. I recommend that all checks be written from the checkbook only.

3. *Maintain a home ledger.* If all records are kept in a checkbook ledger you run the risk of losing it. A home ledger eliminates this possibility and makes record keeping more orderly. Figure A is an example of a typical checkbook ledger form.

CHECKBOOK LEDGER FORM

DATE	CK.#	TRANSACTION	DEPOSIT	WITHDRAWAL	BALANCE

Figure A

USE OF THE CHECKBOOK LEDGER

Note that in the checkbook ledger each deposit and withdrawal is recorded, and the outstanding balance is shown. At the end of each month the ledger is balanced against the bank statement. Also, the total balance in the ledger is then compared to the balance on the budget account sheets.

CHECKBOOK LEDGER

DATE	CK. #	TRANSACTION		DEPOSIT		WITHDRAWAL		BALANCE	
12/1		Deposit	O	$755	00			$755	00
12/5	1105	First Finance Co.	③			$423	00	332	00
12/5	1106	Sam's Supermarket	④			60	00	272	00
12/9	1107	GMAC - Payment	⑤			140	00		
12/15		Deposit	O	755	00			710	00
12/20	1108	Sam's Supermarket	⑥			30	00	280	00
12/20	1109	Tax				40	00	240	00
		...ty Co.	③			70	00	170	00
12/30		Transfer to Savings	O			170	00	-0-	
			O						
			O						
			O						

Balance in checking must equal combined balances on account sheets.

If there are additional deposits or withdrawals from the bank statement recorded in the checkbook ledger, these must also be posted in the appropriate individual account form. For example, a service charge from the bank would be posted as an expense in the checkbook ledger and as a miscellaneous expense in category 12 of the budget.

CHECKBOOK LEDGER

DATE	CK. #	TRANSACTION		DEPOSIT		WITHDRAWAL		BALANCE	
12/1		Deposit	○	$755	00			$755	00
12/5	1105	First Finance Co.	③			$423	00	332	00
12/5	1106	Sam's Supermarket	④			60	00	272	00
12/9	1107	GMAC - Payment	⑤			140	00		
12/15		Deposit	○	755	00			710	00
12/20	1108	Sam's Supermarket	④			30	00	280	00
12/20	1109	Tax...				40	00	240	00
		...ility Co.	③			70	00	170	00
12/30		Service Charge	②			8	00	162	00

INDIVIDUAL ACCOUNT PAGE

Miscellaneous ⑫ $ 38 $ 38
ACCOUNT CATEGORY   ALLOCATION   ALLOCATION

DATE	TRANSACTION	DEPOSIT		WITHDRAWAL		BALANCE	
12/1	Allocation	$ 38	00			$ 38	00
12/15	Allocation	38	00			76	00
12/30	Service Charge			$ 8	00	68	00
12/30	Transfer to Savings			68	00	—0—	

Note that the circle (○) on the checkbook ledger is used to indicate the category to which the check has been allocated in the budget. This is filled in *only* after the check has been recorded in the proper budget category.

ACCOUNTING — ALLOCATION — CONTROL

A budget that is not used is a waste of time and effort. The most common reason a budget is discarded is because it's too complicated.

The system described in this book is the simplest, yet most complete possible.

KEEP IT SIMPLE

The Goal — Establish a level of spending for each category such that more money in does not mean more money to spend, and know where you are with respect to that level at all times.

This budget system is analogous to the old "envelope system." In the past, many employers paid earnings in cash. To control spending, families established an effective system by dividing the available money into the various budget categories (housing, food, clothes, etc.), then holding it in individual envelopes.

As a need or payment came due, money was withdrawn from the appropriate envelope and spent.

The system was simple and, when used properly, quite effective for controlling spending. The rule was simple: When an envelope was empty, there was no more spending for that category. Money could be taken from another envelope, but a decision had to be made — immediately.

Since most families today get paid by check, and since holding cash in the home is not always advisable, a different cash allocation system is necessary.

It is important to know how much *should* be spent, how much is being spent, and how much is *left* to spend in each budget category. To accomplish this, account control pages have been substituted for envelopes. All the money is deposited into a checking account and individual account forms are used to accomplish what the envelopes once accomplished. How much is put into each account (or envelope) from monies received during the month is determined from the Monthly Income & Expenses sheet (Figure B).

MONTHLY INCOME & EXPENSES

GROSS INCOME PER MONTH _____
- Salary _____
- Interest _____
- Dividends _____
- Other _____

LESS
1. **Tithe** _____

2. **Tax**
   (Est.-Incl. Fed.,
   State, FICA) _____

NET SPENDABLE INCOME _____

3. **Housing** _____
   - Mortgage (rent) _____
   - Insurance _____
   - Taxes _____
   - Electricity _____
   - Gas _____
   - Water _____
   - Sanitation _____
   - Telephone _____
   - Maintenance _____
   - Other _____

4. **Food** _____

5. **Automobile(s)** _____
   - Payments _____
   - Gas & Oil _____
   - Insurance _____
   - License/ Taxes _____
   - Maint./ Repair/ Replace _____

6. **Insurance** _____
   - Life _____
   - Medical _____
   - Other _____

7. **Debts** _____
   - Credit Card _____
   - Loans & Notes _____
   - Other _____

8. **Enter. & Recreation** _____
   - Eating Out _____
   - Baby-sitters _____
   - Activities/ Trips _____
   - Vacation _____
   - Other _____

9. **Clothing** _____

10. **Savings** _____

continued on next page

11. **Medical Expenses** _____
   Doctor _____
   Dentist _____
   Drugs _____
   Other _____

12. **Miscellaneous** _____
   Toiletry,
    cosmetics _____
   Beauty,
    barber _____
   Laundry,
    cleaning _____
   Allowances,
    lunches _____
   Subscriptions _____
   Gifts (incl.
    Christmas) _____
   Cash _____
   Other _____

13. **School/Child Care** _____
   Tuition _____
   Materials _____
   Transportation _____
   Daycare _____

14. **Investments** _____

15. **Unallocated**
    Surplus Income[1] _____

TOTAL EXPENSES ▬▬▬

INCOME VS. EXPENSES
Net Spendable Income _____
Less Expenses _____
▬▬▬

[1]This category is used when surplus income is received. This would be kept in the checking account to be used within a few weeks; otherwise, it should be transferred to an allocated category.

Figure B

USE OF THE INCOME ALLOCATION FORM
(refer to Figure D)

The purpose of the income allocation page is to divide net spendable income among the various budget categories. It is simply a predetermined plan of how each paycheck or income source is going to be spent.

Once you have determined from the budget analysis how much can be spent in each category per month, write it in the *Monthly Allocation* column.

Next, divide the monthly allocation for each category (housing, food, etc.) by pay period.

EXAMPLE: Family income is received twice each month. Note that the mortgage payment is made on the 29th of the month so the allocation must be divided in a manner to make sure that adequate funds are available at the time the payment is due. Utility and maintenance payments would have to be made from another pay period.

	ALLOCATION	PAY PERIOD	
HOUSING	$573	$423	$150
FOOD	$200	$100	$100
AUTO	$260	$160	$100
INSURANCE	$ 39	$ 14	$ 25

It is not mandatory that checks be divided evenly. The important thing is that the money be available when a payment is due. Therefore, some reserve funds from the middle-of-the-month pay periods must be held to meet obligations that come due at the first of the month. Failure to do this is a common source of budget problems.

USE OF THE INDIVIDUAL ACCOUNT FORM PAGES
(refer to Figure C)

A separate account form is used for each budget category (housing, food, auto, etc.) just as each had its own envelope under the cash system.

At the top of the page, the proper account title is entered (housing, food, etc.) together with the monthly allocation. Each account sheet has two blanks ($ _____). These are used to write in your allocation for a twice-monthly pay period. If you are paid more frequently, just add more blanks ($ _____). This will help you to remember how much to write in each pay period.

INDIVIDUAL ACCOUNT FORM (portion of Figure C)

| _____ | $_____ | $_____ |
| ACCOUNT CATEGORY | ALLOCATION | ALLOCATION |

The purpose of the account form is to document *all* transactions for the month. The pay period allowance or allocation is shown as a deposit, and each time money is spent, it is shown as a withdrawal.

If funds are left at the end of the month, the account page is zeroed by transferring the money to the savings account. If an account runs short, then it may be necessary to transfer money from savings to the appropriate account. When an account is out of money, a decision must be made concerning how it is going to be treated.

INDIVIDUAL ACCOUNT FORM

	$	$
ACCOUNT CATEGORY	ALLOCATION	ALLOCATION

DATE	TRANSACTION	DEPOSIT	WITHDRAWAL	BALANCE

Figure C

INCOME ALLOCATION FORM

INCOME		INCOME SOURCE/ PAY PERIOD			
BUDGET CATEGORY	MONTHLY ALLOCATION				
1. TITHE					
2. TAX					
3. HOUSING					
4. FOOD					
5. AUTO					
6. INSURANCE					
7. DEBTS					
8. ENTERTAINMENT & RECREATION					
9. CLOTHING					
10. SAVINGS					
11. MEDICAL/ DENTAL					
12. MISCELLANEOUS					
13. SCHOOL/ CHILD CARE					
14. INVESTMENTS					
15. UNALLOCATED SURPLUS INCOME					

Figure D

HOW TO USE THE BUDGET SYSTEM

A good budget system should be kept as simple as possible while still accomplishing its goal: *to tell you if you spend more than you allocated each month.* Remember that this system is analogous to using envelopes. If a specific amount of money is placed in the envelopes each month, you will know at a glance whether or not your budget balances. Obviously, with some non-monthly expenses to be budgeted, the ledger system has to be a little more complicated, but don't *over-complicate it.*

To help you better understand how to use the budget system, we will take one category (housing) through a typical month's transactions (see example here and page 176):

INCOME ALLOCATION FORM

INCOME		INCOME SOURCE/ PAY PERIOD			
		1st	15th		
BUDGET CATEGORY	MONTHLY ALLOCATION	1041	1041		
1. TITHE	$208	$104	$104		
2. TAX	365	182.50	182.50		
3. HOUSING	573	423	150		
4. FOOD	200	100	100		
5. AUTO	260	160			
6. INSURANCE					

Figure D (example)

175

INDIVIDUAL ACCOUNT FORM

$$\underline{\quad HOUSING \quad ③ \quad}\ \$\underline{\quad 423 \quad}\ \$\underline{\quad 150 \quad}$$
ACCOUNT CATEGORY   ALLOCATION ALLOCATION

DATE	TRANSACTION	DEPOSIT	WITHDRAWAL	BALANCE
12/1	Allocation	$423 00		$423 00
12/5	Mortgage		$423 00	-0-
12/15	Allocation	150 00		150 00
12/29	Electric		70 00	80 00
12/30	Transfer to Savings		80 00	-0-

Figure C (example)

This illustration shows a typical family budget in which the gross income of $2,082 per month is received in two pay periods of $1,041 each.

PAY ALLOCATION—The two checks have been divided as evenly as possible among the necessary categories. For example, the tithe is paid each pay period (remember, it is based on gross income). The housing allocation of $573 is divided: $423 in the first pay period, $150 in the second.

HOUSING ALLOCATION—On the first pay period, a deposit of $423 is noted on the account page. On the 5th of the month, the mortgage is paid and noted as a withdrawal, leaving a balance of $0.

Each transaction is noted similarly until, at the end of the month, a balance of $80 is left. This balance is then transferred to savings, as are month-end balances from the other account pages (food, savings, etc.). Hence, each account starts at zero the next month.

Many people prefer to leave the surplus funds from each category in their checking account rather than transfer them to a savings account. This is fine provided that you can discipline yourself not to spend the money just because it's easily accessible. Often the total cash reserves in checking are enough to qualify for free checking privileges, which more than offset any loss of interest in a savings account.

NOTE: In many cases, the housing account may have to carry a surplus forward to make the mortgage payment if it comes due on the 1st of the month.

POTENTIAL PROBLEM AREAS

CASH WITHDRAWALS—Many times miscellaneous expenditures are made with personal cash. In establishing a budget, it is important to develop some rules for self-discipline.

1. Separate personal cash into categories identical to the account pages. Use envelopes if necessary, but avoid spending gas money for lunches and grocery money for entertainment.
2. When all the money has been spent from a category (entertainment, lunches, etc.), *stop spending!*
3. Don't write checks for amounts in excess of actual purchases to get cash. Write another check and note it as "cash, personal."

CATEGORY MIXING—Don't try to make the record-keeping more complicated than necessary. This system should require no more than 30 minutes per week to maintain. If you choose to develop more detailed breakdowns of expenses and savings, wait until the budget has been in use at least six months.

AUTOMATIC OVERDRAFTS

Many banks offer an automatic overdraft protection service. Thus if you write a check in excess of what you have in your account, the bank will still honor it. On the surface this looks like a helpful service. However, it has been my experience that overdraft protection tends to create a complacent attitude about balancing the account and encourages overdrafting. Since these charges are accrued to a credit account, you will end up paying interest on your overdrafts. Avoid overdraft protection until your budgeting routine is well established. Hopefully by then it will be unnecessary.

BUDGETING ON A VARIABLE INCOME

One of the most difficult problems in budgeting is how to allocate monthly spending when your income fluctuates, as it often does on commission sales. The normal tendency is to spend the money as it comes in. This works great during the high income months but usually causes havoc during the lower income months.

Two suggestions will help anyone living on a fluctuating income: *First,* always separate any business-related expenses such as car maintenance, meals, living accommodations, etc., from your normal household expenses. I recommend a separate checking account for business expenses and separate credit cards, if needed.

Second, you need to estimate what your (low) average income for one year will be and generate your monthly budget based on the "average" income per month. As the funds come in, they need to be deposited in a special savings account and a salary drawn from the account. The effect is to ration the income over the year in relatively equal amounts that can be budgeted.

Remember that if you are self-employed, you will need to budget for payroll taxes on a quarterly basis. Failure to do this will result in a rather unpleasant visit with representatives of the Internal Revenue Service.

If you are beginning your budget during one of the lower income months, you may have to delay funding some of the variable expenses such as clothing, vacations, dental, etc. These can be funded later when the income allows.

WHAT IF YOU ARE PAID EVERY TWO WEEKS?

If you are paid every two weeks rather than twice monthly, you will have two extra paychecks a year. I recommend using these paychecks to fund some of the non-monthly expenses such as car repairs, vacations, clothing, etc. The same would be true of tax refunds, bonuses, and gifts.

APPENDIX B

WILLS AND TRUSTS

The vast majority of Americans do not have a will or a trust. If they died today they would leave the distribution of their assets to the state. This represents poor stewardship. Most people recognize the need to have a will, but they never get around to having one drawn. Many others had a valid will at one time, but either the witnesses have died or the state laws have changed, invalidating their wills.

Regardless of the reason, the simple truth is that if your will cannot be probated (proved) in court, it is worthless. In most states the effect is swift and certain. The state agency assigned to handle intestate (having no legal will) properties will divide them among the surviving heirs (after extracting probate costs, state inheritance taxes, and federal inheritance taxes).

Rather than spend a few hundred dollars in attorney costs, many of these estates will spend several times that in court costs before the assets are distributed. A simple will can avoid these problems. For more complicated estates, consisting of larger assets, a trust may be more advantageous.

Perhaps the best way to discuss this issue is in a question-and-answer format. This will help you to understand what kind of estate planning is best for your family.

Question 1: Can I draft my own will without having to pay an attorney?
Answer: Yes, you can in the majority of states. A self-drawn will is called a holographic will. Holographic means that it is a document written totally in the handwriting of the person drafting it. The rules governing holographic wills vary by state, and you must thoroughly understand the laws of your state to insure your will is probatable (provable) in court.

Question 2: What if one of my witnesses has died?
Answer: In order for a will to be probated, the judge may

require the will to be verified. If you used only two witnesses and the state requires a minimum of two, both must be alive. It is always best to use three or even four witnesses that you know well. If less than the required minimum are still alive, you will need to amend your will with a codicil to have other witnesses verify it.

Question 3: Should I keep my will in a safety deposit box?

Answer: If you do so you need to be sure that someone else has access to the box. Since a safety deposit box cannot be opened except by court order, the process can be lengthy and expensive in the event of your death. If no one else knows about the box, it may never be recovered. I suggest that you name your spouse as an authorized signatory, as well as your attorney or accountant.

Question 4: Do I need a new will if I change residences from one state to another?

Answer: Possibly. You need to have an attorney in the new state review your will to insure it conforms to that state's laws.

Question 5: What if I own property in more than one state?

Answer: Generally, your estate is governed by the state in which you reside at the time of your death. Thus a valid will drawn in your state can control the distribution of assets in another state, even if that state's laws are different.

Question 6: Do I need a will if my wife and I hold all of our property in joint tenancy?

Answer: Yes. Joint tenancy means that the surviving tenant or spouse owns the property upon the death of the other tenant, but if there are assets owned outside the joint properties, they would not be covered. In our generation this is common where they may be large settlements due to negligent deaths, such as an automobile accident.

Bear in mind also that some states tax joint property as if the deceased owned it outright, while others tax a proportionate interest in it. You will need to check with an attorney in your state to determine how jointly owned properties are taxed, if at all.

Also, if both of you are killed in a common accident, the last surviving tenant would be declared intestate (without a valid will). The estate would be subject to dual taxation and additional legal costs.

Question 7: Who can I name as my estate executor?
Answer: You can name anyone you desire to act as executor of your will and estate. That person's duties are to probate the will and distribute the assets accordingly. You may choose to name more than one person to serve as executor and should always name at least three alternates in the event that one cannot or will not serve.

Unless you stipulate otherwise, many states require an out-of-state executor to post a bond. Some require a bond equal to the value of the estate. Since your estate will have to bear this cost, you may want to waive the requirement to post bond.

Bear in mind that if you use a professional executor, there will be a fee involved. This can vary from an hourly fee to a percentage of the estate value. Any such fees should be clearly spelled out in a contract and then attached to your will or trust.

Question 8: When is a trust better than a will?
Answer: A trust is a legal contract to manage someone's assets, before and after death. There are two basic types of trust: a "living trust," known as an inter-vivos trust, and a "testamentary" trust, meaning that it commences upon the death of the person.

A living trust is drafted and implemented while the assignee is still living. Within these trusts is another division: A trust may be "revocable" or "irrevocable." If it is revocable, the assignee reserves the right to modify or cancel the trust and to remove or substitute property as long as he/she is alive. An irrevocable trust means exactly that: It is irrevocable and cannot be changed once in force. Nor can the property assigned to the trust be recovered by the donor.

Question 9: What is the advantage of a trust?
Answer: A trust is not a public document, as is a will, and does not require probate. Thus, a trust insures a greater measure of privacy.

Also, since a trust is not probatable, there are no probate costs associated with assets held in a living trust. Since a testamentary trust is created within a will (normally), the will must first be probated before the trust becomes effective. A testamentary trust therefore does not avoid probate costs on the assets of the assignee.

If the living trust is irrevocable, the assets held in trust are not subject to estate taxes, except to the extent that the assignee retains an interest in them. Literally, the assets are given to trust and become trust property. There may be gift taxes due on assets assigned to a trust for the benefit of others.

Question 10: Can I draft my own trust?
Answer: There are will and trust "kits" available in most bookstores today. These purport to explain how to draft your own will or simple trust. While it is legal for a layman to draft a holographic will or trust, I personally don't advise it. Once you are deceased, it's too late to change the will or trust if it doesn't pass the test. As the old saying goes, you can be "penny wise and pound foolish."

Question 11: How much tax will my estate have to pay?
Answer: That depends on the value of your estate at death. Through a marital deduction allowance, each spouse can leave the other an unlimited amount of assets. However, assets left to someone other than a spouse are subject to estate (death) taxes. (See the sections on federal and state estate taxes.)

Question 12: When are the taxes due?

Answer: Usually within six months of death, the state will require an appraisal of the estate. The taxes are due and payable at that time, although in practice both the state and federal tax collectors will normally work out a plan to convert the assets necessary to pay the taxes so that the estate doesn't suffer a severe dilution through a forced sale.

Liquidity (cash) in an estate is very important since the taxes must be paid in cash. Otherwise, assets must be sold to satisfy the tax collectors. If the assets cannot be sold through normal market channels, the estate may be auctioned off at a substantial loss.

Question 13: What if I change my mind after I make a will?

Answer: You can change your will through the use of a codicil (supplement). The codicil is subject to the same laws of probate, so it is important that it be drafted properly. Attach all codicils to the original will and store them together. Remember that only the original will or codicil is probatable, so protect them carefully.

Often when a spouse dies, the surviving spouse is numbed into inactivity. Usually the shock of the loss requires that others help the widow(er) with the essential planning necessary to get her life back in order. This brief section is written for those who will help the bereaved.

TAKING THE MYSTERY OUT OF PROBATE

Probating (proving) a will is not complicated in most instances. It is merely a matter of taking the original document to the court of the ordinary in the county or province where the deceased resided (primary residence) and having it officially verified and recorded. Unless the judge determines that there is some potential legal flaw in the will, that's all there is to it.

If the will is challenged by an heir or beneficiary, then the judge will require that the witnesses swear to the will's validity. This can usually be done by deposition (sworn statement) without the witnesses appearing in court.

Once the will is probated, the court will empower the executor to fulfill the requirements of the deceased.

THE DUTIES OF THE EXECUTOR

The executor of a will is literally the one who executes the wishes of the deceased. This may include reading the will to the heirs, dispersing property or funds, selling assets, and any other functions specified in the will.

The executor may or may not receive compensation from the estate. If the will expressly provides for compensation from the estate, the judge will grant it. If the will does not prohibit compensation, the executor may appeal to the probate judge for reasonable compensation. The expenses associated with executing the will are generally covered by the estate.

An executor may not divert estate assets to him- or herself unless the terms of the will so specify. The executor is a steward (manager) of the estate until the terms of the will are fully satisfied. In a simple estate this may be as short as a few days or weeks, while in a complicated estate this may take several years.

Choosing a competent and worthy executor is very important. It has been my observation in counseling that the executor can make the distribution of assets a pleasant or irritating experience for all involved. Multiple executors may be named to oversee the terms of the will, and may be granted joint or mutually exclusive authority.

Normally the executor will also be charged with appraisals and other duties necessary to settle the estate. He or she will usually be empowered to write checks and disperse funds for estate expenses under court supervision.

It is always a good policy to appoint successor executors in the event that those named cannot or will not serve in the assigned capacity. I recommend naming at least one professional executor, such as an attorney, accountant, trust officer, etc., for just such a circumstance.

THE DUTIES OF A TRUSTEE

Unlike the duties of an executor, which are over once the terms of the will are satisfied, the trustee's duties are usually much longer term. A trust document is normally meant to handle and disperse assets for a long period of time and requires periodic accounting and tax reports. Thus, naming a trustee is somewhat more complicated and should be done after careful evaluation of the skills and experience necessary.

In the case of a living trust, the donor to the trust can often serve as trustee, although the degree of control he or she exercises may adversely affect the taxable status of the assigned assets. It is generally best to have someone other than the donor serve as trustee if the donor reserves an interest in the trust.

In the case of a testamentary trust, since it is created upon the death of the donor, the trustee must be specified in the trust document.

The trustee can be empowered to buy and sell for the estate and transact any business necessary in the name of the trust. The powers of the trustee are always spelled out in the trust document itself. Co-trustees can be named, and successors should always be specified. As in the case of an executor, a professional trustee should always be named in the event that no other named trustees choose to serve.

APPENDIX C

SOCIAL SECURITY BENEFITS

In the event of the death of someone covered by Social Security benefits, it is important to file for these benefits in a timely fashion. Usually the benefits will be paid retroactively, but the more timely the filing, the simpler it will be to collect what is due the beneficiaries.

If you have never requested an evaluation of the benefits due you or your spouse from Social Security, I would suggest doing so as soon as possible. While there is no longer a statute of limitations during which corrections to your account must be made, the sooner any errors are discovered, the simpler the correction process will be.

To check on the allocation for Social Security, you will need a copy of form SSA-7004 (sample copy provided in Figure 1), available by calling the Social Security office in your community or calling toll-free 1-800-234-5772.

WHO IS COVERED?

Social Security earnings are credited to a person's account based on a "quarter of coverage" system. Before 1978, workers earned a quarter of coverage if they were paid $50 or more in a calendar quarter. The amount is determined at the end of each year and has increased annually to keep pace with average wages. The requirement for 1990 was $520 of earnings per calendar quarter.

FULLY INSURED

"Fully insured" is a status you reach after accumulating 40 quarters of coverage. A person employed for at least 10 years in jobs covered by Social Security can normally assume to be fully insured. Fully insured means full benefits!

CURRENTLY INSURED

"Currently insured" is a status you achieve after accumulating at least six (6) quarters of coverage in the 13-quarter

SOCIAL SECURITY ADMINISTRATION

Request for Earnings and Benefit Estimate Statement

To receive a free statement of your earnings covered by Social Security and your estimated future benefits, all you need to do is fill out this form. Please print or type your answers. When you have completed the form, fold it and mail it to us.

1. Name shown on your Social Security card:

   First   Middle Initial   Last

2. Your Social Security number as shown on your card:

   ☐☐☐ - ☐☐ - ☐☐☐☐

3. Your date of birth:

   Month   Day   Year

4. Other Social Security numbers you may have used:

   ☐☐☐ - ☐☐ - ☐☐☐☐
   ☐☐☐ - ☐☐ - ☐☐☐☐

5. Your Sex: ☐ Male ☐ Female

6. Other names you have used (including a maiden name):

7. Show your actual earnings for last year and your estimated earnings for this year. Include only wages and/or net self-employment income subject to Social Security tax.

   A. Last year's actual earnings:

   $ ☐☐☐,☐☐☐.☐ ☐
     Dollars only

   B. This year's estimated earnings:

   $ ☐☐☐,☐☐☐.☐ ☐
     Dollars only

8. Show the age at which you plan to retire: _____

9. Below, show an amount which you think best represents your future average yearly earnings between now and when you plan to retire. The amount should be a yearly average, not your total future lifetime earnings. Only show earnings subject to Social Security tax.

   Most people should enter the same amount as this year's estimated earnings (the amount shown in 7B). The reason for this is that we will show your retirement benefit estimate in today's dollars, but adjusted to account for average wage growth in the national economy.

   However, if you expect to earn significantly more or less in the future than what you currently earn because of promotions, a job change, part-time work, or an absence from the work force, enter the amount in today's dollars that will most closely reflect your future average yearly earnings. Do not add in cost-of-living, performance, or scheduled pay increases or bonuses.

   Your future average yearly earnings:

   $ ☐☐☐,☐☐☐.☐ ☐
     Dollars only

10. Address where you want us to send the statement:

    Name

    Street Address (Include Apt. No., P.O. Box, or Rural Route)

    City   State   Zip Code

    I am asking for information about my own Social Security record or the record of a person I am authorized to represent. I understand that if I deliberately request information under false pretenses I may be guilty of a federal crime and could be fined and/or imprisoned. I authorize you to send the statement of my earnings and benefit estimates to me or my representative through a contractor.

    Please sign your name (Do not print)

    ▶

    Date   (Area Code) Daytime Telephone No.

    ABOUT THE PRIVACY ACT
    Social Security is allowed to collect the facts on this form under Section 205 of the Social Security Act. We need them to quickly identify your record and prepare the earnings statement you asked us for. Giving us these facts is voluntary. However, without them we may not be able to give you an earnings and benefit estimate statement. Neither the Social Security Administration nor its contractor will use the information for any other purpose.

    ☐ SP

Form SSA-7004-PC-OP1 (6/88) DESTROY PRIOR EDITIONS

Figure 1
187

period ending with the quarter in which you die or become disabled. Generally, a currently insured person may be entitled to disability benefits but not retirement benefits.

RETIREMENT BENEFITS

To qualify for retirement benefits you must be at least 62 years old and fully insured. Generally, if one spouse is receiving old-age benefits, the other is also entitled to benefits upon reaching age 62. A spouse is eligible for benefits before 62 if he or she is caring for a child who is entitled to receive benefits. If you wait until age 65 before applying for old-age benefits, you're entitled to receive 100 percent of your entitlement. This full entitlement is called your "Primary Insurance Account" (PIA). However, you can apply for a reduced amount of benefits at age 62.

If you claim retirement benefits before age 65, the amount of your monthly benefit is permanently reduced by certain percentages, depending upon your age when the benefits are claimed. If the benefits start at exactly age 62, the reduction is about 20 percent of your full Primary Insurance Account (PIA). For each month you wait after reaching age 62, a formula is used to determine your benefit amount. If you continue working past the full-benefit age of 65 and are not receiving benefit payments, monthly benefits are increased by 3 percent for each year after you reach age 65.

When you receive retirement benefits, your children under the age of 18 are also eligible for benefits if they're single and living at home. A child's benefits are usually discontinued upon reaching age 18 (age 22 if a full-time student, but these student benefits are scheduled to be phased out).

A mother's benefit payments based on her having a child in her care will normally stop when that child reaches age 16 (unless the child is disabled) even though the child is a full-time student and receives benefit payments in his or her own right until age 18.

DISABILITY BENEFITS

When you qualify as being a disabled worker, you're entitled to receive monthly benefit payments in the same amount you would have been paid had you been retired under normal conditions. Meeting the requirements for disability benefits is not easy, but there are exceptions for persons disabled before reaching age 31 and for the blind. To qualify as disabled, you must meet *all* of the following conditions:

a. Be under the age of 65 and have enough Social Security coverage when the waiting period for disability benefits begins. At present there is a five-month waiting period, and payments start in the sixth full month of disability.

b. The degree of your disability must be severe enough to prevent you from doing any substantial gainful work.

c. The disability must last (or be expected to last) for at least 12 months or to result in death.

d. You must have accumulated at least 20 quarters of coverage under the system in the 40-quarter period which ends in the quarter you became disabled.

Disability benefits may also be paid to disabled children past the age of 22 if they were disabled before reaching age 22 and have remained disabled. Persons entitled to disability benefits for 24 straight months also qualify for Medicare benefits.

SURVIVOR BENEFITS

When a person covered by Social Security dies, monthly benefits may be payable to certain survivors. The amounts paid are based on the person's full Social Security entitlement (full PIA), even though the person started receiving benefits before reaching age 65.

For a fully insured worker, survivor benefits are payable to a widow or widower, or surviving divorced wife or husband, age 60 or over (ages 50-59 if disabled), as well as to the worker's dependent parents who are age 62 or over.

Benefits paid to a surviving spouse because he or she cares for a child will be discontinued when the child reaches age 18, even if the child is a full-time student receiving benefit payments in his or her own right.

LUMP-SUM DEATH BENEFIT PAYMENTS

When a fully or currently insured worker dies, a one-time lump-sum death benefit of $225 is payable to his or her surviving spouse if that spouse is eligible (or would be eligible except for age) for monthly survivors' benefits. If there's no eligible surviving spouse, the lump-sum death benefit can be paid to a surviving child who is eligible for child's benefits.

MEDICARE BENEFITS

Medicare is a two-part insurance program covering the hospital and medical care costs for persons age 65 or older who are entitled to receive Social Security. Part A covers hospital insurance benefits, and Part B covers medical insurance benefits.

APPLYING FOR SOCIAL SECURITY

Your Social Security benefits are not automatically started when you become eligible to receive them. You must apply for each benefit to which you're entitled. Since it takes time to process the paperwork, you should apply for benefits at least three months before your actual entitlement date.

When applying for benefits, you'll need to have your Social Security card (or proof of your number) and be able to prove your age with either a birth or baptismal certificate. A copy of your marriage license is necessary when applying for survival or spousal benefits. When applying for child's benefits, you'll need a copy of his or her birth certificate.

ESTIMATING SOCIAL SECURITY BENEFITS

Because the computation methods are so complex, it's almost impossible to accurately determine the exact amount of Social Security benefits you will qualify to receive at some future point in time. In 1990, the average retired worker was paid $558; the average retired couple (both over age 65) received $958; the average widowed mother with two children received from $1,113 to $1,156; and the average disabled worker received $550.

Let the Social Security Administration do the estimate for

you! They've started a new service that gives you a detailed accounting of how much you've paid into the system and estimates of your retirement benefits at ages 62, 65, and 70. Call their toll-free number, 1-800-234-5772, and ask for Request Form SSA-7004. After completing and returning the form, you should get a reply in five to six weeks.

TABLE FOR ESTIMATING AMOUNTS OF SOCIAL SECURITY BENEFITS

Average Monthly Wage	Old-Age Benefit Age 65	Old-Age Benefit Age 62	Dependent Spouse Age 65	Dependent Spouse Age 62	Average Monthly Wage	Old-Age Benefit Age 65	Old-Age Benefit Age 62	Dependent Spouse Age 65	Dependent Spouse Age 62	Average Monthly Wage	Old-Age Benefit Age 65	Old-Age Benefit Age 62	Dependent Spouse Age 65	Dependent Spouse Age 62
$83	144	115	72	54	609	495	396	248	186	1250	710	568	355	266
92	1158	127	79	59	641	517	413	258	194	1275	716	573	358	269
101	172	138	86	65	660	527	421	263	198	1300	722	578	361	271
107	184	147	92	69	685	536	429	268	201	1325	729	583	364	273
122	195	156	105	79	705	544	435	272	204	1350	735	588	367	276
146	210	168	105	79	725	551	441	276	207	1375	741	593	371	278
169	224	179	112	84	745	559	447	280	210	1400	747	597	373	280
193	239	191	119	90	770	567	454	284	213	1425	753	602	376	282
216	253	202	127	95	790	573	459	287	215	1450	759	607	379	285
239	268	215	134	101	810	580	464	290	218	1475	764	612	382	287
258	280	224	140	105	835	588	470	294	221	1500	770	616	385	289
281	294	235	147	110	860	596	477	298	223	1525	775	620	388	291
300	306	245	153	115	885	604	483	302	226	1550	781	625	390	293
323	320	256	160	120	910	611	489	306	229	1575	786	629	393	295
342	331	265	166	124	930	618	494	309	232	1600	792	635	396	297
365	346	277	173	130	955	626	501	313	235	1625	797	638	399	299
389	361	288	180	135	980	634	507	317	238	1650	803	642	401	301
412	375	300	188	141	1000	640	512	320	240	1675	808	647	404	303
436	388	311	194	146	1030	648	519	324	243	1700	814	651	407	305

Figure 2

TABLE FOR ESTIMATING AMOUNTS OF SOCIAL SECURITY BENEFITS

Average Monthly Wage	Old-Age Benefit Age 65	Old-Age Benefit Age 62	Dependent Spouse Age 65	Dependent Spouse Age 62
459	402	322	201	151
478	413	330	206	155
501	427	341	213	160
524	440	352	220	165
548	454	363	227	170
563	464	371	232	174
577	473	379	237	178
591	483	387	242	181

Average Monthly Wage	Old-Age Benefit Age 65	Old-Age Benefit Age 62	Dependent Spouse Age 65	Dependent Spouse Age 62
1050	654	523	327	245
1075	661	529	331	248
1100	669	535	334	251
1125	676	540	338	253
1150	683	546	341	256
1175	690	552	345	259
1200	696	557	348	261
1225	703	562	352	264

Average Monthly Wage	Old-Age Benefit Age 65	Old-Age Benefit Age 62	Dependent Spouse Age 65	Dependent Spouse Age 62
1725	819	655	410	307
1750	825	660	412	309
1775	830	664	415	311
1800	836	669	418	313
1825	841	673	421	315
1850	847	677	423	318
1875	852	682	426	320
1900	858	686	429	322

APPENDIX D

VETERANS' BENEFITS

Generally, to qualify for VA benefits, a veteran's active duty service must have been terminated under conditions other than dishonorable. While an Honorable or General discharge will qualify a veteran for most benefits, a Dishonorable discharge usually disqualifies a veteran for most benefits. A Bad Conduct discharge may enable the veteran to qualify for some benefits, depending on the VA's determination of facts surrounding the member's discharge.

SURVIVORS' AND DEPENDENTS' EDUCATION

If a veteran dies or is permanently and totally disabled as a result of military service, his or her surviving spouse and dependent children may qualify to receive financial help for educational purposes. These benefits are also available to a spouse and dependent children of a member who is a prisoner of war or is missing in action for more than 90 days.

Training can be in an approved vocational school, business school, college, professional school, or a business having an apprentice or on-the-job training program. It also includes training in a secondary school, by correspondence, or in an educational institution offering farm co-op programs.

Normally the length of training cannot exceed 45 months of schooling or the equivalent of 45 months if enrolled on a part-time basis. A child's marital status is no barrier to receiving these benefits, but the remarriage of a surviving spouse will end his or her entitlement unless the new marriage is terminated by death or divorce.

DEPENDENCY AND INDEMNITY BENEFITS

The payment of Dependency and Indemnity Compensation (DIC) was originally intended to assist the surviving spouse and dependent children of a veteran whose death resulted from a service-connected disability or cause. Changes in the law have broadened the scope of DIC benefits to include the survivors of certain veterans whose deaths do not meet the earlier (and more stringent) rules.

WHEN DEATH IS DUE TO A NON-SERVICE-CONNECTED CAUSE

DIC payments can be authorized to certain survivors of veterans who were totally disabled from a service-connected cause, but whose deaths were not the result of that service-connected cause or disability. Benefits are payable if the veteran was:

a. Continuously rated as totally disabled for a period of 10 or more years; or

b. If so rated for less than 10 years, was so rated for at least five years from the date he or she was discharged.

Benefit payments are authorized for the veteran's surviving spouse, to any unmarried children under the age of 18 (under 23 if they're students), and to certain helpless children.

DEATH PENSION FOR SURVIVING SPOUSES

Based on financial need and ability to qualify, a veteran's surviving spouse and unmarried children under 18 (under 23 if students) may be entitled to a monthly VA pension.

For the survivors to qualify, the deceased veteran must have had at least 90 days of service and must have been separated or discharged under conditions other than dishonorable — unless the separation was due to a service-connected disability. If the veteran died while serving on active duty, but the death was not in the line of duty, benefits may be payable if he or she had completed at least two years of honorable active military service.

Insofar as the surviving spouse is concerned, he or she must have married the veteran at least one year prior to death unless a child resulted from the marriage.

VA BURIAL BENEFIT

The Veterans' Administration will furnish a headstone or marker to memorialize or mark the grave of a veteran buried in a national, state, or private cemetery. The VA also provides markers to eligible family members interred in a national or state veterans' cemetery.

If death is not service-connected, the VA provides a burial allowance of $300 if the veteran was entitled at the time of death to VA compensation or died in a VA medical facility. A plot or interment allowance of $150 is also available if the veteran is entitled to the burial allowance, served during a war period, or was discharged or retired from service because of a disability which was incurred or aggravated in the line of duty. A veteran buried in a national or other federal cemetery, however, is not eligible for this plot allowance. The plot allowance may be paid to a state if the veteran was buried in a state veterans' cemetery.

If the death is service-connected, the VA will pay an amount not to exceed $1,000 in lieu of the burial and plot allowance. The VA will also provide an American flag for use in covering a casket; a reimbursement is likewise available for part of the cost of a private headstone or marker bought after the veteran's death. (The current amount is $71.)

For further information, contact the Veterans' Administration, 810 Vermont Avenue, (40) N.W., Washington, D.C. 20420.

APPENDIX E

INSURANCE BENEFITS

Perhaps the most important assets available to most widows/widowers are the proceeds from a life insurance policy on their spouse. This section is meant to provide some idea of what amount of life insurance is adequate, and to help in the decision about which insurance is the best for your situation. No one type of insurance is right for everyone, and as a family's situation changes, the needs change also.

LUMP SUM OR ANNUITY?

Often I have been asked by a grieving spouse (more commonly a widow) about whether it would be best for her to take a cash settlement from the insurance company or a lifetime annuity. To be honest, it is very difficult to make that kind of decision without a great many supporting facts. It is very difficult to ask a grieving spouse to make such a decision for at least the first year. I usually recommend that she accept the cash payment, then place the proceeds in a very secure investment for the long term.

WAIT ONE FULL YEAR

Above all else I would recommend to any recent widow: Don't make any critical financial decisions during the first year. I have seen many people do so, and they usually regretted most of those decisions later.

DETERMINING INSURANCE NEEDS

HOW MUCH INSURANCE DO I NEED AND CAN I AFFORD?

The amount of life insurance a family needs depends on many variables, such as family income, the ages of the children, the ability of the wife to earn an income, Social Security status, the standard of living you hope to provide, and outstanding debts.

The Insurance Needs Worksheet (pages 200-1) will assist you in determining what the requirements are. The requirements will then have to be weighed against the budget. If the budget dollars are limited, it will be necessary to get as much insurance as possible for the available dollar.

PRESENT INCOME PER YEAR

How much income is being provided by the breadwinner of the family? The goal is to provide for the family so that they may continue the same living standard they enjoy under this income.

PAYMENTS NO LONGER REQUIRED

Family expenses should drop as a result of the death of the breadwinner. For example, a second car may no longer be required; less income (or different income) will mean less taxes; activities or hobbies would not be an expense; investments or savings may be reduced or stopped.

INCOME AVAILABLE

The breadwinner's death may initiate income from some other sources. Social Security income will depend on one's eligibility which, in turn, is determined by the time in the system, amount of earnings, and ages of spouse and dependent children. Income may also be available from retirement plans, investments, annuities, etc.

The income-earning potential of the wife is a definite asset to the family. Ages of the children are a factor here. A minimum insurance program should provide time for obtaining or sharpening job skills if necessary.

ADDITIONAL INCOME REQUIRED TO SUP-PORT FAMILY

The income presently being earned, less the payments no longer required and less the income available, results in the income that needs to be supplied in order for the family to continue living on the same level enjoyed through the income of the husband.

INSURANCE REQUIRED TO PROVIDE NEEDED INCOME

If provision could be made in an "ideal" manner, the insurance money invested at 10 percent would return the needed amount of income to the family. To find the required amount of insurance, multiply the income required to support the family by 10.

> Example: $7,000 additional income is required to support the family; $7,000 x 10 = $70,000. $70,000 in insurance invested at 10 percent would provide the needed funds.

LUMP SUM REQUIREMENTS

In addition to the insurance required to produce the regular sustained income, lump sums may be required for specific purposes (e.g., college education). Those needs should be determined and added to the total amount of insurance.

Are funds needed to pay off the home mortgage? This should be discussed as a part of the family plan. If mortgage payments are being made under the existing income, then this could be continued under the sustained income provision. Since paying for the home would significantly boost the insurance requirement, this will also raise the amount that must be spent for insurance.

ASSETS AVAILABLE

Determine the assets that are available for family provision. Subtract this amount from the desired amount of insurance.

Equity in a home can be counted as an asset only if the survivors plan to sell it.

TOTAL INSURANCE NEEDED

The total tells how much insurance is needed. This must be balanced against how much can be spent for insurance. If the insurance dollars are limited, it will be necessary to get as close to the plan as possible with those dollars. Term insurance with its lower initial premiums probably offers the best opportunity for adequate provision with fewest dollars.

The plan should also include instructions as to how the insurance money is to be used.

NOTE: Insurance needs should be reviewed periodically. Family changes (i.e., new additions, children becoming employed or leaving home, inflation changes, income changes, etc.) should prompt an insurance review.

INSURANCE NEEDS WORKSHEET

PRESENT INCOME PER YEAR
⎯⎯⎯⎯
Line 1

PAYMENTS NO LONGER REQUIRED
Estimated Living Cost (for Husband) ⎯⎯⎯⎯
Life Insurance ⎯⎯⎯⎯
Savings ⎯⎯⎯⎯
Investments ⎯⎯⎯⎯
Taxes ⎯⎯⎯⎯
⎯⎯⎯⎯⎯⎯⎯⎯⎯⎯⎯⎯⎯ ⎯⎯⎯⎯
⎯⎯⎯⎯⎯⎯⎯⎯⎯⎯⎯⎯⎯
Total = ⎯⎯⎯⎯
Line 2

INCOME REQUIRED TO SUPPORT FAMILY (Line 1 − Line 2) =
⎯⎯⎯⎯
Line 3

INCOME AVAILABLE
Social Security ⎯⎯⎯⎯
Wife's Income ⎯⎯⎯⎯
Retirement Plans ⎯⎯⎯⎯
Investments ⎯⎯⎯⎯
⎯⎯⎯⎯⎯⎯⎯⎯⎯⎯⎯⎯⎯ ⎯⎯⎯⎯
⎯⎯⎯⎯⎯⎯⎯⎯⎯⎯⎯⎯⎯
Total = ⎯⎯⎯⎯
Line 4

ADDITIONAL INCOME REQUIRED TO SUPPORT FAMILY
(Line 3 − Line 4) =
⎯⎯⎯⎯
Line 5

INSURANCE REQUIRED TO PROVIDE THE NEEDED INCOME
(Line 5 x 10) =

_____
Line 6

LUMP SUM REQUIREMENTS
Debt Payments _____
Funeral Costs _____
Estate Tax & Settlement Costs _____
Education Costs _____

_____

_____

Total = _____
Line 7

TOTAL FUNDS REQUIRED
(Line 6 + Line 7) =

_____
Line 8

ASSETS AVAILABLE
Real Estate _____
Stocks & Bonds _____
Savings _____

_____ _____

_____

Total = _____
Line 9

TOTAL INSURANCE NEEDED
(Line 8 − Line 9) =

_____

APPENDIX F

BUYING A CAR

In our society owning a car is a fact of life. To be sure, there are those, particularly in large urban areas, who are able to get about using public transportation, but the lifestyle of today's average family makes owning at least one car a practical necessity. So, having this need for a car as a "given," what is the most economical way of obtaining it?

PRELIMINARY STEPS

1. EXAMINE YOUR MOTIVES.

Let's face it. The majority of new automobile sales in the U.S. are made because of the buyer's wants, not needs. In fact, a significant portion of people who are shopping for a car—new or used—simply do not need it. Often they are just tired of their car; it looks old and out of date, or it needs major repairs to put it back into top condition, or their neighbors or coworkers have acquired new cars. We have been programmed to think that if any of these conditions exists, we are justified in acquiring another—preferably new—car.

Cars do wear out, and everyone will eventually find himself or herself in the position of having to get another car. Everyone, however, would do well to examine their motives first, because so often the notion to buy a car springs from the emotional rather than the rational side of our human nature.

2. DETERMINE YOUR NEEDS.

Having examined your motives, the next step is to determine your needs. Luke 14:28 says, "For which of you, when he wants to build a tower, does not first sit down and calculate the cost, to see if he has enough to complete it?" Most everyone would naturally like to be sitting behind the wheel of a shiny new automobile. But have they calculated the cost? They need to consider not only the question of whether they can afford it, but also whether buying a new car is the best stewardship of their family's hard-earned money.

Costs (payments, insurance, maintenance, etc.) for a mid-range new car commonly run in excess of $300 a month. That kind of expense can wreck the average family's budget. Sure, they may be able to make the monthly payments, but the other major budget categories, like food and clothes, will begin to suffer, and since these are major needs, the family will inevitably go into debt to obtain them.

The average family needs to buy a good-quality, reliable, used car. Of course the size, style, age, and appearance of the car will vary from family to family.

3. BECOME AN INFORMED BUYER.

Doing your homework before you begin can help you find the car best suited to your needs. Consumer advocacy groups and publications such as *Consumer Reports* report on the safety, maintenance, and value of the various car models. Remember too that cheaper does not always mean a better deal.

Friends and family members are also a good source of information. Talk with owners of cars similar to the model you are considering to see if they are satisfied.

SHOPPING FOR A USED CAR

FRIENDS

Once you have determined the type of car you want and can afford, the next step is to find the car. Go to your closest friends first. Let them know you're looking for a car. Find out if there is a Christian family in your church that has a car to sell that will fit your need. Before most Christians will sell their car to somebody they know, they will either tell him everything that is wrong with the car or else have it fixed. By purchasing directly from the owner, you can learn the history of the car and usually negotiate the best possible price.

LEASING COMPANIES

A second good source of used cars is a leasing company. Many of these companies keep their cars one or two years and then resell them. Most of these cars have been routinely maintained, have low "highway" mileage, and are usually available for a fair price. Often a car obtained from a leasing company will come with a one-year warranty.

BANKS

A third good source is from your local banker. Let him know that if he obtains a really good car as a repossession (where the bank has to recover the car), you are interested in buying it. Be aware that a repossessed car probably will need some repairs since its owner most likely couldn't afford to keep it maintained properly. Make sure that you have some money in reserve for this purpose.

CAR DEALERS

Dealers have the largest selection of used cars available. A used car which was locally owned can be a good deal, especially if you are able to contact the previous owner to see if there are any hidden problems with the car.

ADVERTISEMENTS

A fourth source is advertisements through newspapers and similar publications. The difficulty in going through this source is that you don't know the seller, and the seller doesn't know you. Unfortunately, there are a lot of unethical, dishonest people out there that have cars for sale.

Before buying any used car, it is advisable to write out an affidavit saying, "I swear that the car that I am selling, to my knowledge, has no obvious defects or rust, and that the mileage on the odometer is accurate." Have the seller sign it (before a notary if possible). Most honest people won't object, and most dishonest ones won't sign it.

Finally, have a mechanic check the car you are purchasing for defects or problems which may not be obvious to you, such as hidden rust, signs of having been in an accident, and engine problems. The dollars you spend upfront having a mechanic look at the car can save you much grief and expense later on.

Appendix F

ABOUT FINANCING

The best way to finance a car is *not* to finance it at all! It is always the best policy to save the money and pay cash for your car. Auto financing is poor stewardship at the very best. But, assuming that there are those who, for some reason or another, feel they must finance the purchase of their car, there are some basic guidelines which should be followed:

1. DO NOT FINANCE THROUGH THE CAR DEALERSHIP IF AT ALL POSSIBLE.

Arranging a loan through a bank or other financial institution can allow you to negotiate with the dealer on a "cash basis." When you do arrange a loan, be sure it is a simple interest loan with no pay-off restrictions. Then at least you have the option to become debt free in a shorter period of time.

2. DO NOT TRADE IN YOUR OLD CAR – SELL IT INSTEAD.

If a car dealer can sell your car and make a profit, so can you. It certainly takes more time and effort to sell your car, but it is worth it. Advertise your car by a notice in the newspaper or a sign in the window. Provided your car is in reasonable shape, it shouldn't take very long to sell.

3. IF YOUR OLD CAR IS NOT PAID OFF, KEEP IT UNTIL IT IS.

If you trade in a car with a mortgage on it, you are simply taking your current debt and refinancing it into a new car, effectively doubling the amount of interest you have been paying on your old mortgage.

ANSWERS TO QUESTIONS ABOUT BUYING A CAR

SHOULD I BUY AN EXTENDED WARRANTY ON MY NEW CAR?

If you are considering an extended warranty, there are several questions you need to ask. First, does the warranty cover a period of time or a number of miles that is not covered under any implied warranties? Second, does the extended warranty cover parts and labor, or parts only? Third, does the price of the extended warranty seem reasonable in relation to the price of the parts covered?

If an extended warranty covers five years or 50,000 miles, then the average driver will really only get coverage for approximately three years since the average person drives more than 10,000 miles per year. A better warranty would cover five years or 100,000 miles.

If only parts are covered, the cost of labor is usually so great that the owner will not get the full benefit of buying the extended warranty unless each part covered is more expensive than the relative cost of the warranty.

HOW MUCH OF OUR FAMILY'S BUDGET SHOULD BE DESIGNATED FOR CAR EXPENSES?

About 15-17 percent of your *net spendable income* (income after deducting tithes and taxes) should be allotted for automobile expenses. That includes payments, gasoline, oil, maintenance, and insurance.

WHAT ARE SOME WAYS I CAN CUT MY CAR EXPENSES?

First, you can save money on car insurance. The average family's car is more than three years old. The only kind of insurance to have on that car is liability, which is required by law. Shop and compare prices on liability insurance. Second, you can save money on tires. Go to a tire dealer and ask if he sells "take-offs," which are tires that have been taken off a new car because the buyer wanted a different kind. Take-offs are nearly new and may be half the price of brand new tires.

Third, consider starting a car maintenance co-op or join an existing one. A typical co-op involves a group of Christians who meet regularly at a church parking lot to perform routine maintenance and car repairs for one another.

Preventive maintenance will save on towing charges due to unexpected breakdowns on the highway. Check your local library for books on car ownership that offer other money-saving tips.

WHAT ABOUT LEASING A CAR?

Leasing a car often seems attractive to those who cannot otherwise afford a new car because it involves little or no down payment. However, that means that the whole cost of a leased vehicle is financed for the entire lease period. Also, a lease is a contract to pay that is just as binding as a purchase contract and places the lessee in a position of surety.

For example, if the lessee runs into unexpected financial problems, he cannot sell the car outright because he does not hold the title. The leasing company does. Even if the leasing company would arrange for the sale of the car (and it is under no obligation to do so), almost always the amount owed on the lease is more than the car is worth, leaving the lessee with no car and still owing more money!

WHAT IS SURETY?

The Book of Proverbs has over 20 references to the principle of surety. "Surety" is taking on an obligation to pay for something without an absolutely certain way to pay for it.

To keep from becoming surety, the best policy is to never borrow. But if you do borrow, make sure that the item for which you borrowed is total collateral and that you would not be liable for any deficiency beyond that.

SUMMARY

Honestly evaluate your real need for a car. If you determine your need justifies a purchase, buy a used car. Generally speaking, it is a much better buy. Shop for value, not always the lowest price. Save for your car and pay cash. However, if you must borrow, go through an institution other than the dealership. Arrange for a simple interest loan with no pay-off restrictions. Then negotiate with the dealer on a cash basis. Finally, rather than trading your old car in, sell it yourself.

APPENDIX G

HOUSING

Since the cost of buying or renting suitable housing for your family is perhaps the greatest expense you'll ever incur, you must study your personal situation, research the possibilities, and pray for the Lord's guidance in order to make an educated decision about finding what's right for you.

CONSIDER THE VARIABLES

Before you decide whether to rent or buy a house, determine how much you can afford to spend. If you are not actively living on a budget, you should make this your first step. *The Financial Planning Workbook* (Moody Press) is excellent in helping you set up a written financial plan.

Although your financial situation will be the major factor in determining what type of housing you need, there are other variables that must be considered. Prayerfully give these questions some thought:

1. Is your job secure enough to take on a mortgage? If not, consider renting instead of buying a house.
2. How long do you plan on staying in the area? If you know you will be staying in the community for an extended time—five to seven years at least—home ownership may be a good option.
3. What is the economy like in the area you are considering? Is the area growing substantially and will the house appreciate? You don't want to be stuck with a house that you can't sell because of a poor economy.
4. What is the cost of living in the new area? If it is high, it will definitely affect your budget and may change the amount you can afford for housing.

After answering these questions, take the amount you can spend for housing and determine if house payments, including taxes and insurance, would be equal to or less than rental payments for a similar house in the same area. If they would be, then buying a home may be a wise choice.

Appendix G

BIBLICAL PRINCIPLES TO CONSIDER

Borrowing: God doesn't prohibit borrowing, but He certainly does discourage it. In fact, every biblical reference to it is a negative one. Consider Proverbs 22:7, "The rich rules over the poor, and the borrower becomes the lender's slave." Homeowners who lose their jobs and are unable to keep up with the payments find out firsthand what it's like to be in the position of a slave. Remember, borrowing is literally a vow to repay, and God requires that we keep our vows.

Surety: Another biblical principle that affects you when you borrow money is "surety." Proverbs 17:18 says, "A man lacking sense pledges, and becomes surety in the presence of his neighbor." Surety is simply taking on an obligation to pay later without a certain way to pay it. For example, if you buy a house and put up a 5 percent down payment and finance 95 percent, then the real estate market only needs to decrease 5 percent for you to risk being caught in surety. But if you put 20-30 percent down on a house and finance 80-70 percent, then your risk of being caught in surety is not as great. If you're going to borrow to buy, accumulate enough for a sizable down payment.

The best way to avoid surety, however, is to make sure that any money you borrow is fully collateralized. Suppose you bought land that cost $10,000, and you put $1,000 down and borrowed $9,000. The terms of your contract should stipulate, "If I can't pay for this land, I give you the right to take the land back, and keep all the money I've paid in, but I'm released from all personal liabilities." A statement that releases you from personal liability for the loan is called an "exculpatory clause." Unfortunately, most institutions hold you personally responsible for mortgages and don't allow exculpatory clauses in their contracts. Surety is a biblical principle, not a law, but it will certainly come to haunt you when you can least afford it.

RENTING A HOUSE

If you have decided that renting a house is a better option for you at this time, there are several things to consider. First, decide what type of dwelling you want to rent. You can rent a house, apartment, townhouse, mobile home, or even a room or suite in someone's house. The people in your church are often a good source of information about availability, location, and cost of rentals around the area.

Types of leases: There are two main types of leases. One is a month-to-month lease, and the other is a lease for a specified amount of time — usually six months or one year. The month-to-month lease is great if you aren't sure how long you will be in the area or if you are waiting for a house to be finished. The problem with this type of lease is that the rent can be raised with simply a 30-day notice. You can avoid this problem with a six-month or yearly lease. The rental price is renegotiated at the end of the lease term, and you can choose to stay and pay more or move out.

Deposits: A security deposit is usually required when you sign a lease. This deposit can be retained by the owner if you damage the property while you are renting or if you have to move before your lease is up. A cleaning, pet, or key deposit may also be required. These are usually refunded when you turn in your keys and the owner inspects the property.

Renter's insurance: The purpose of renter's insurance is threefold. It covers the value of your furniture and personal belongings, protects you from being sued by the owner's insurance company if there is damage to the property — i.e., grease fire or water damage, and it covers the liability if someone else is hurt on the property because of your or your children's negligence — i.e., someone falls or trips over a toy and is injured. Content and liability insurance usually costs about $100 to $150 a year and is well worth it, unless you can afford to replace all your belongings and have plenty of money on hand to cover exposed liabilities.

BUYING A HOUSE

If you've determined that purchasing a house fits into your budget and is in your best interest long term, you can begin to look at the options available to you. You might consider these different types of dwellings: houses — including a new house or rebuilding a "fixer-upper," condominiums, or mobile homes.

Houses: First you will need to decide whether you want to purchase a new or used house. The advantages of building a new house are that you can design your house to fit your individual needs and locate it where you want it. The disadvantages of a new house are, with few exceptions, those who build a new house end up spending more money than they planned. Changes made while the house is being built cost a lot of money, and it takes considerable time and mental effort to oversee the construction of a new house.

The advantages of buying a used house are that you know exactly what it is going to cost, and you can get more extras. Used houses usually come with curtains, curtain rods, towel racks, lights in the closets, light bulbs, an established lawn, shrubbery, and, occasionally, appliances. Make sure the contract states exactly which items will come with the house. The disadvantages of a used house are that any time a house has been lived in, it will have some wear and tear. The older the house, the more things that will need repair. You should always check the heating and air conditioning, roof, hot water heater, and appliances to see if they are in working condition. You may choose to hire someone to do this for you. Then you can decide whether to purchase the house as is or back out of the deal.

The fixer-upper or handyman's special: Another alternative is a fixer-upper. This type of a house can be purchased at a relatively lower cost than other previously owned houses. But you will need to take into consideration the additional funds required outside of the normal housing allocation for repairs. Be sure to check the house thoroughly, including foundation, plumbing, and wiring, so you know exactly what is wrong with the house before you buy it. If you have the skills and don't mind doing the repairs, you can make a nice profit when you sell it.

Condominiums: Another option is a condominium. You need to be aware of some additional costs involved above the purchase price, such as maintenance fees and club fees—if you wish to use the amenities available in a private community. Be aware that the maintenance fees are subject to change each year, and you have no control over them. This is not a bad option, especially if you don't want to bother with yard work.

Mobile homes: Although some people won't consider living in manufactured housing because of preconceived notions about this type of housing, many couples (and single parents) have purchased mobile homes and think they are great. It gives them better housing than they could afford otherwise and satisfies the needs of their families.

The major disadvantage of manufactured housing is the depreciation. A new mobile home will lose about 25 percent of its total value when it leaves the sales lot. Consider purchasing a previously owned mobile home, because someone else has already taken the depreciation.

PURCHASE OPTIONS

Now that you've decided what type of house you want to buy, you need to decide how to pay for it. In order to serve God in the very best way, the goal of all Christians should be to become debt free — including their house. If you choose to borrow money to purchase the house, you should make it your goal to pay the house off as soon as possible. There are several ways to do this that will be discussed later.

Pay cash: The best way to buy a house is to pay cash if you are financially able. The idea of owning a house debt free is not a new one; in fact, it's quite ancient. Most families used to own their houses, and those who didn't were abnormal. Those who couldn't afford the large house they wanted simply bought a smaller house, put a great deal of time and effort into it, improved its value, sold it and then upscaled.

Institutional loans (through banks, savings and loans, credit unions, or mortgage companies): If you have to borrow to buy your house, an institutional loan is perhaps the most common type of loan, although it may not necessarily be the best type for you. It's very important to shop around with this type of loan, because there are so many variables. As you enter the marketplace of house buyers, you should know what type of loans are available to you and what additional costs are associated with each.

Fees and contracts: Most institutional loans require a down payment — usually 5-20 percent, but you can and should put more down if possible — and various "closing costs." Closing costs can include loan origination fees, points, attorneys' fees, survey fees, appraisal fees, PMI (private mortgage insurance), real estate commissions, credit reports, title search fees, and more. These fees can add up to quite an expense — several thousand dollars — and should be researched thoroughly when considering any loan. Many times the seller may pay for some or all of the closing costs.

If your offer to purchase the house is subject to selling your present house, getting financial approval, or waiting on results from various inspections, including radon gas testing, termite inspections, appliance and structural inspections, or water testing, make sure these contingencies are spelled out in the contract.

Fixed-rate mortgages are an excellent form of home loan. You know exactly what the interest rate and monthly mortgage payment will be and if it will fit into your budget. Although a fixed-rate loan will have slightly higher interest rates than other types of loans, it will not change during the life of the loan. You will know that the terms are for the next 15 or 30 years. Shop around for the lowest interest rate, since they do vary from institution to institution and from week to week.

Adjustable rate mortgages (ARM) are not a bad form of home loan, provided you can get an interest rate lower than the prevailing fixed rate and the loan contains a cap on the maximum increase during the life of the loan. These loans fluctuate with the economy; therefore it's very important to know exactly how high the interest rate could go. Most ARMs begin with an interest rate that's a percentage point or two below current fixed-rate loans, then they are "adjusted" every year after that. This makes it possible for more couples to "qualify" for these types of loans, but makes it hard to establish exactly how much to budget for housing expenses from year to year.

Make sure you understand the terms before you choose this type of loan. For example, if you can get an 11 percent ARM with a 5 percent cap—or a maximum rate of 16 percent—and the current fixed rate is 13 percent, you would be better off accepting the ARM than the fixed-rate mortgage. However, you need to figure out what your monthly payment would be if the interest rate rose to 16 percent. Would that payment fit into your budget comfortably?

One last point to consider on adjustable rate loans is the duration of the loan. Many of these loans are short-term loans that carry a balloon payment (typically due in seven years). Therefore, I don't advise them for most people, unless you know you can pay off the house in that amount of time. There is no guarantee you'll be able to renegotiate another loan you can afford, and you could lose your house.

"Payday" mortgages are designed to increase the frequency of your loan payments. Instead of paying a monthly payment, the house buyer pays one-half the monthly payment every other week or one-quarter of the payment every week. Since more of the payment is applied to the principal, equity is accrued at a faster rate. This will consequently reduce the life of the loan and the borrower reaps the benefits of paying less interest and paying off the house mortgage early. Some lenders don't offer this type of loan because they lose interest. However, this financing option is becoming more popular due to increasing competition.

Compare a $60,000 Mortgage at 12%

	P/I	Life of Loan (Yrs.)	Interest Paid	Interest Saved
Weekly	$154.29	18.79	$ 90,809.33	$71,362.20
Bi-weekly	$308.59	19.04	$ 92,752.05	$69,429.15
Conventional	$627.27	30	$162,181.20	-0-

An **assumable mortgage** is an existing mortgage that is assumed by the buyer at the existing terms of the seller's loan. Assumable mortgages benefit the buyer because the interest rate and mortgage payment are usually lower than current rates. Check to see if there is an assumption fee and if the loan will be assumable if you sell the house to someone else.

Government financing: Purchasing a house with a loan subsidized by the government may be a matter of concern to some people. Although there are no biblical principles that specifically apply to this subject, it is my personal opinion that Christians should not look to the government for help, but rather to God. By depending on the government to supply more and more of our basic needs, I fear this will eventually take away from our trust in God. If you have prayed about it and still feel you should take advantage of the subsidized loan, then by all means follow the conscience the Lord gave you.

There are several types of government loans that may be obtained through your local banking institution. VA, FHA, and state-bonded programs are attractive to house buyers because of the low interest rates and the low down payment required. Be careful not to get yourself into surety with these types of loans.

Seller financing (land sales contract, trust deed, etc.): Another way to purchase a house is for the seller to finance the house for the buyer. This provides a steady income to the seller, and the buyer usually gets the financing for a percent or two lower than current interest rates and saves on closing costs. Be sure a qualified attorney draws up all legal papers so there is no question about the terms of the sale.

Equity sharing is an excellent way for a couple to get help in purchasing a home and for an investor to receive a healthy return on a relatively small investment. This is the way it works. A couple needing help in obtaining funds for a down payment on a mortgage locates an investor willing to provide a certain portion of those funds. A written agreement is drawn up which defines the amount of years the house will be retained by the buyers and the amount of equity that will be paid to the investor once the house is sold. Usually the investor will receive his full investment back plus 50 percent of any profit.

A provision should be made so that if the couple wants to keep their home after a period of years, the investor will be repaid with a predetermined amount of interest on his original loan. In order to avoid any differences, a good Christian attorney should be involved in the preparation of any equity-sharing plan.

Parent-assisted financing: I believe it is our responsibility as parents to help our children reasonably—though not take all the burdens off them. For example, a parent puts up the down payment for his son or daughter to buy a house. The home is in joint ownership—the parent owns part of it, and the child owns part. The parent then rents the house back to the children. The parent receives the income, depreciates the house, and takes it off his taxes, while the child rents it, retains partial ownership, and profits from the eventual sale. The child should provide the repairs and maintenance needed. This method benefits both parent and child and may also be used by Christians willing to help young couples (nonfamily members) get their first house.

Parents with substantial savings may also choose to be the lender for their children. This method will save money on closing costs and can be a source of retirement income for the parents. Make sure, however, that the children are mature enough to be responsible for this generosity and that they do not take advantage of you. All legal forms should be drawn up and on record so there are no questions if the parents or the children pass away or in the event of default. Parental financing should be viewed by both parties with the same financial commitment and the same consequences as any other type of financing.

SELLING YOUR HOUSE
If you are on the other side of the coin and are selling a house instead of purchasing one, there are certain things you should

know. First, you must decide who is going to sell your house.

By owner: You can elect to sell your house yourself in order to save the cost of a real estate agent's commission. This means you will advertise it yourself and must be available to show the house to interested buyers. Be knowledgeable about selling your house. Know what other houses in your area are selling for and understand what you must do when someone contracts to buy the house. Have a qualified attorney review all offers before you sign anything.

By real estate agents: You may choose to have an agent sell the house for you. This will give you greater exposure in the real estate market. It may save you time and money because the agent can advertise, use the Multiple Listing Service, and show the house while you are at work. You will have to pay the agent's commission — around 5-10 percent of the selling price — if your house sells. Have the broker explain every offer that is made for the purchase of your home. You may choose to have an attorney review all offers if you are not knowledgeable about real estate.

OTHER CONSIDERATIONS WHEN SELLING YOUR HOME

Tax consequences: If you sell your house and buy another that costs less than the house you sold, you must pay a capital gains tax on the difference between the two houses. However, there are allowances for selling costs and improvements that can reduce the gain. You may postpone tax payment if you buy a more expensive house within two years. There is also a one-time exclusion on capital gains for those more than 55 years old. You may want to contact a professional accountant or tax advisor for additional help.

Continued liability: You can be held liable for any loan a buyer assumes from you if the buyer defaults, unless you obtain a total release from liability. Contact the lending institution for more information about obtaining one of these releases. Check to see if there is a fee involved.

Earnest money contracts: When someone is genuinely interested in buying your house, they will submit a contract and earnest money. This is a deposit on the house so you won't sell it to anyone else while the potential buyer is getting financing approved, selling his house, or awaiting inspection results. At this time you should be willing to explain any problems or situations the buyer should know about the house. Not only will it save the buyer some headaches down the road, but you will be setting a wonderful Christian example. This is also the time to declare which items will be included in the purchase price. Some items to consider are appliances, curtains, swing sets, firewood, or maintenance equipment. You may desire to present a counter offer showing any terms of their offer you are unwilling to accept.

QUESTIONS ABOUT REFINANCING
Should I refinance to obtain a lower interest rate? If you are considering refinancing your house to take advantage of lower interest rates, determine if it will actually save you money by figuring the dollar amount of interest you will save compared to the costs involved in refinancing. Some banks will require new title searches, surveys, and appraisals to refinance your loan. If you can easily reclaim these expenses through the savings in interest within a few years, refinancing is for you. You will usually benefit through refinancing if the new interest rate is at least 3 percent lower than your present mortgage.

Should I get a home equity loan (second mortgage) to pay off my consumer debts? Proverbs 3:27-28 says, "Do not withhold good from those to whom it is due, when it is in your power to do it. Do not say to your neighbor, 'Go, and come back, and tomorrow I will give it,' when you have it with you." If you can't pay your bills on a regular basis and you have the means to pay those bills, God requires that you do whatever it takes to pay them off. Unfortunately, borrowing more money, especially against the equity in your home, doesn't usually solve the problem. It only treats a symptom of the problem. You must treat the problem itself. If you are having problems with your credit cards, cut them up. Establish a budgeted payment plan and repay each creditor. Work at paying off the smaller debt first, then the next, and so on. Remember, the borrower becomes the lender's slave.

OTHER QUESTIONS ABOUT REAL ESTATE

What happens if the bank forecloses on my house? Although foreclosure is a serious problem, it does not mean God has washed His hands of you. As a result of losing a house, you will learn a costly yet valuable lesson on the danger of surety. And although you may not be held legally responsible for the difference between the amount of your mortgage and the price the lender receives from the sale of the house, you are morally responsible for this debt. When you enter into a contract, you are bound by your word to fulfill its intent. Remember Psalm 37:21. Once the foreclosure has been finalized, work out a payment plan for the balance which will fit into your adjusted budget.

The lender will always have the option to file a deficiency judgment against you. He may retain this right for several years. Check your state laws. He also may choose to release you from the deficiency debt. He is the master and has this right. You must commit to pay the deficiency and do whatever the lender requests.

If you are fortunate enough to deed the home to the lender instead of being foreclosed on, you may avoid paying anything, but you will still lose the house and equity. If you have fallen behind on your payment or must move quickly, make every effort to sell your house even if you have to take a loss. Since foreclosed houses are generally sold at auction for much less than fair market value, you can often sell it for more, thus reducing the amount you must pay back.

What type of insurance should I have on my house? Most lending institutions require that you have enough insurance to cover the amount of the mortgage. A homeowner's insurance policy is a comprehensive insurance plan covering the home, its contents, and any liability associated with the property. Usually the homeowner's policy is the least expensive way to insure a dwelling. You can get a fire policy only, but it isn't as comprehensive as a homeowner's policy. Shop around before you buy any kind of insurance because there can be a significant amount of difference in the cost of insurance from one company to another.

If you are going to buy a condominium or mobile home, most insurance companies provide specialized insurance for these types of dwellings.

Should I have life insurance to cover my house? It is very wise for a family to have life insurance to pay their house off. This insurance is commonly called mortgage life insurance.

Mortgage life insurance is usually sold through the lender where you received your house loan. This can be a very expensive way to purchase life insurance. A decreasing term insurance policy through your local insurance agent may be less expensive.

The best option would be to determine what your total life insurance needs are and include your house loan balance with this. By purchasing one policy versus several you will save money. As your need for death protection diminishes, you can reduce your coverage.

What types of prepayment options are available? After you have made your regular monthly payment, any additional funds you put toward your mortgage go directly to the principal, exclusive of any interest. Therefore, the next month you're paying slightly less interest and slightly more principal on the unpaid balance. Each month that you prepay part of the principal, a greater amount goes toward the principal the following month, since your regular payment amount stays constant. By this prepayment method, a $60,000 mortgage at 10 percent for 30 years can be reduced by approximately $68,500 and 16 years by prepaying an additional $100 per month.

You may want to write two separate checks, one for the regular monthly payment, and one for the additional principal — write "principal" on this check to make sure there is no confusion at the lending institution.

$60,000 Mortgage at 10%

	P/I	Life of Loan (Yrs.)	Interest Paid	Interest Saved
Conventional	$526	30	$129,360	-0-
Additional $100	$626	16	$ 60,818	$68,542
Additional $50	$576	20	$ 78,240	$51,120
Additional $25	$551	23.8	$ 97,586	$31,774

Another prepay option available is a "payday" mortgage. Refer back to the paragraph under "Institutional Loans."

Before making any prepayments on your mortgage, check with your lending institution about any penalties and request an annual amortization schedule to monitor the reduction in your principal balance.

Many families will be able to make extra monthly principal payments—$50, $100—and pay their loans off earlier than scheduled. This may be the simplest option for most families.

Is buying foreclosed homes ethical? Are we guilty of robbing the poor (condemned in God's Word) when we take over foreclosed homes? A Christian must first ask himself, "Did I help to cause the problems that generated the foreclosure?" In other words, did you lend somebody money they could not pay back and then foreclose on the home? If so, you would be guilty of robbing the poor.

The second question that a Christian has to ask is, "Am I being fair?" Have you willfully taken advantage of someone else's misery? In practical fact, these people are going to lose their houses regardless of whether you buy them out of foreclosure, because the bank is going to foreclose. As long as you did not generate the foreclosure, there is nothing scripturally wrong with buying a foreclosed house. If you can get to the family before they get into foreclosure, you could save them some money they might lose otherwise. Remember what Paul wrote in Philippians 2:3, "Do nothing from selfishness or empty conceit, but with humility of mind let each of you regard one another as more important than himself."

Am I too old to buy a house? One of the essential foundation blocks of a biblically oriented financial plan is a debt-free home. This should be the goal of all Christians, but particularly so for retirees. Anything can happen to this economy. It may be a collapse or hyperinflation brought on by printing massive amounts of money to avoid a depression. Either way, you can lose whatever is indebted. A debt-free home is yours, not the lender's.

Personally, I would do whatever is necessary to become debt free at age 65 or older. If it were necessary to sell a larger house and pare down expenses by buying a smaller, debt-free house, I would also do that. We are a nation of debtors, and eventually we will grasp the meaning of Proverbs 22:7, "The rich rules over the poor, and the borrower becomes the lender's slave."

To a great extent your circumstances will determine whether or not you should buy a house. Don't put yourself in jeopardy just to "own" a house. If you have a "certain" way to pay for the house, then it may be a good idea. However, if you are older, don't depend on your health or your job to make mortgage payments. Both can easily be lost as you get older.

Should I pay off my mortgage and lose the tax deduction? People who borrow to purchase houses often believe that the tax breaks they receive justify the interest that is paid. Those who are in the 28 percent tax bracket and pay $1,000 in interest in a year may receive a $280 tax credit. This obviously shows that $720 went into someone else's pocket—the lender's. The best alternative is to pay off your home mortgage as early as possible and not only save the interest, but accumulate a sizable savings. This far outweighs any tax deductions you may receive from paying interest.

APPENDIX H

FEDERAL ESTATE TAXES

While the federal estate tax code has been greatly improved over the last decade, poor planning can still result in some significant tax liabilities. The current federal estate tax ranges from 37-60 percent. But for the majority of estates, this will represent no real liability since the tax begins with estates that have a net worth of $600,000 or more. Also, all assets left to a surviving spouse are exempt from any tax.

The greatest potential tax liability usually involves estates where both spouses die in a short time frame or where there is no surviving spouse. In these instances the estate will be comprised of all assets in which the deceased had any interest, including real properties, insurance, revocable trusts, pension-profit sharings, assets, etc.

Gifts made in excess of the gift tax exemption of $10,000 per year per person or $20,000 for a couple are also potentially taxable in the estate. In addition, the courts have traditionally held that all gifts made within three years of death can be included in the final estate evaluation if such gifts are deemed to have been made in contemplation of death. Generally the evidence to the contrary consists of an established pattern of giving in previous years.

After the amount of the estate (or gift) has been reduced by the various authorized deductions or exclusions, the amount of tax can be tentatively determined by using the rates in the Unified Rate Schedule for Estates and Gift Taxes (Figure 1-a, page 224). Your authorized tax credit is then applied, further reducing the taxable amount. The amount of credit is shown in Figure 1-b.

The following example is given to show how to use the information in these tables:

You leave an estate which, after taking applicable deductions and/or exclusions, totals $800,000. From Figure 1-a you can see that the tax is $248,300 plus 39% of the amount above $750,000

Unified Rate Schedule for Estates and Gift Taxes			
If the Amount Is			
Over This	But Not Over	Tentative Tax Is	On Excess Amount Over
$ 0	$ 10,000	0 plus 18%	$ 0
10,000	20,000	1,800 plus 20%	10,000
20,000	40,000	3,800 plus 22%	20,000
40,000	60,000	8,200 plus 24%	40,000
60,000	80,000	13,000 plus 26%	60,000
80,000	100,000	18,200 plus 28%	80,000
100,000	150,000	23,800 plus 30%	100,000
150,000	250,000	38,800 plus 32%	150,000
250,000	500,000	70,800 plus 34%	250,000
500,000	750,000	155,800 plus 37%	500,000
750,000	1,000,000	248,300 plus 39%	750,000
1,000,000	1,250,000	345,800 plus 41%	1,000,000
1,250,000	1,500,000	448,300 plus 43%	1,250,000
1,500,000	2,000,000	555,800 plus 45%	1,500,000
2,000,000	2,500,000	780,800 plus 49%	2,000,000
2,500,000	3,000,000	1,025,800 plus 53%	2,500,000
3,000,000	10,000,000	1,290,800 plus 55%	3,000,000
10,000,000	21,040,000	5,140,800 plus 60%	10,000,000
21,040,000	....	11,764,800 plus 55%	21,040,000

Figure 1-a

Unified Credit Against Gift and Estate Taxes		
Tax Year	Amount of Tax Credit	Equivalent Exemption
1982	$ 62,800	$ 225,000
1983	$ 79,300	$ 275,000
1984	$ 96,300	$ 325,000
1985	$ 121,800	$ 400,000
1986	$ 155,800	$ 500,000
1987 & Later	$ 192,800	$ 600,000

Figure 1-b

(39% of $50,000 = $19,500). The tax now totals $267,800. However, Figure 1-b shows that your unified tax credit is $192,800. When that is subtracted from $267,800, your total tax comes to $75,000.

Of course, determining the actual amount of taxes owed is often much more complicated than this example, and it's a good idea to let a professional financial planner or tax accountant help reduce the tax liability of your estate as much as possible.

APPENDIX I

STATE DEATH TAXES

When most people think about taxes that are taken out of an estate, they typically think about estate taxes. In reality, only 18 states now have estate taxes. The others use a combination of either death taxes or pick-up taxes.

The amount each state can collect from an estate varies widely, with some states taking only the deductible amount allowed from the federal inheritance tax. This last category is called "pick-up" tax since it is the amount picked up from the federal taxes and represents no additional cost to the heirs.

The federal estate tax code exempts all assets left to a surviving spouse and $600,000 in assets left to all other beneficiaries. However, that same exemption does not always apply to the taxes levied by a state. As of 1990, several states still levy a tax on spousal inheritance.

The amount an estate will be required to pay in state death or inheritance taxes can affect the heirs significantly since the taxes must be paid in cash. Sometimes it is economically beneficial to relocate your primary residence in light of the potential taxes due. Figure 1 (page 226) shows a breakdown of state taxes as of 1990. Naturally these can and will be adjusted periodically. You can obtain a current quotation of the taxes levied by your state by writing the state tax commissioner's office.

State	Death tax ($) On $600,000 estate left to:	
	Spouse	Child
Alabama	None	None
Arizona	None	None
Arkansas	None	None
California	None	None
Colorado	None	None
Connecticut	$0	$37,875
Delaware	0	31,250
Dist. of Columbia	None	None
Florida	None	None
Georgia	None	None
Hawaii	None	None
Idaho	None	None
Illinois	None	None
Indiana	0	24,950
Iowa	0	39,825
Kansas	0	21,750
Kentucky	0	45,370

State	Death tax ($) On $600,000 estate left to:	
	Spouse	Child
Louisiana	$17,050	$17,050
Maine	None	None
Maryland	6,000	6,000
Massachusetts	23,500	55,500
Michigan	0	33,700
Minnesota	None	None
Mississippi	0	1,400
Missouri	None	None
Montana	0	0
Nebraska	0	5,850
Nevada	None	None
New Hampshire	0	0
New Jersey	0	0
New Mexico	None	None
New York	25,500	25,500
North Carolina	0	7,000
North Dakota	None	None

State	Death tax ($) On $600,000 estate left to:	
	Spouse	Child
Ohio	$2,100	$30,100
Oklahoma	0	17,725
Oregon	None	None
Pennsylvania	36,000	36,000
Rhode Island	7,900	12,400
South Carolina	0	33,000
South Dakota	0	41,250
Tennessee	0	0
Texas	None	None
Utah	None	None
Vermont	None	None
Virginia	None	None
Washington	None	None
West Virginia	None	None
Wisconsin	0	56,250
Wyoming	None	None

Figure 1

APPENDIX J

CHECKLIST OF IMPORTANT DOCUMENTS

WILLS

Will For	Dated	Attorney	Location of Will

POWER OF ATTORNEY

Power of Attorney For	Power Given To	Date	Locationn of Document

BIRTH CERTIFICATES

Certificate For	Date of Birth	Certificate Number	Location of Certificate

DEATH CERTIFICATES

Certificate For	Date of Death	Certificate Number	Location of Certificate

MARRIAGE LICENSES

License For	Date of Marriage	Certificate Number	Location of Document

DIVORCE DECREES

Divorce Decree For	Date of Divorce	Decree Number	Location of Document

SOCIAL SECURITY RECORDS

Social Security Records/Card For	Social Security No.	Date Received	Location of Document

REAL ESTATE RECORDS

Records For Property Located At	Type of Record	Dated	Location of Document

AUTOMOBILE RECORDS

Title & Registration For Vehicle	Title Number	Dated	Location of Document

LIFE INSURANCE POLICIES

Policy on Life Of	Policy Number	Company	Location of Document

BANK, SAVINGS & LOAN, OR CREDIT UNION RECORDS

Name of Institution	Type of Account	Account Number	Location of Document

SAFETY DEPOSIT BOXES

Box Registered In Name Of	Name of Institution	Box Number	Location of Keys

CHURCH RECORDS

Type of Record	Record For (Name)	Date of Event	Location of Document

MILITARY RECORDS

Type of Record	Record For (Name)	Date of Event	Location of Document

OTHER IMPORTANT PAPERS

Type of Record	For	Dated	Location of Document